PRAISE FOR PICTURE THEM NAKED..

"I had the tremendous pleasure to receive a preview copy of Jennifer Burrows' book. Seeing the title I was sceptical, but immediately relieved when I started reading. Jennifer put the title right away into perspective — and how she did. Wonderful storytelling combined with practical take-aways; I would have wanted that book when I started my speaking career ten years ago. Chapter after chapter filled with nuggets — if you only thoroughly apply two or three of them, your speaking will profit so much. Congratulations Jennifer. Really enjoyed it."

Martin Laschkolnig, www.martinlaschkolnig.com, *International Keynote Speaker, Director of the board of German Speakers Association, Board Member of the Global Speakers Federation, Working in Europe with Jack Canfield, author of The Success Principles and Co-Founder of 'Chicken Soup for the Soul' series.*

"Even as a professional public speaker, I got an enormous value from 'Picture Them Naked'. I learned things that I can immediately apply to improve my own speaking. Easy to read, entertaining but mostly incredibly empowering ... a great book and a must read for anyone who currently speaks, needs to or wants to speak to groups."

Andrew Jobling, www.andrewjobling.com.au, *author "Dance Until It Rains"*

"Jennifer Burrows' 'Picture Them Naked' is a gem of a book. It is easy to read, filled with personal stories, anecdotes and excellent speaking tips for both the experienced and novice presenter. Thanks Jen for sharing your wisdom and for the practical suggestions contained within the book."

Stephen Pauley, *Founder, Be First Class Limited*

"DIY and self-help books on presentation skills are constantly flooding bookshop shelves and covering Amazon.com these days, thankfully 'Picture Them Naked' is different. Rather than pushing a single angle or just one set of skills, Jennifer Burrows has brought together 18 presentation and entertainment professionals whose continued success — and often their livelihood — depends on their ability to present and engage with their audience and move them to TAKE ACTION. Real situations, real stories, real skills, real techniques — that the reader can start using immediately. Yes, right away! A great read for beginners and those of us with some presentation experience under our belts."

Fiona Fell, Founder and Lead Strategist, Leads To Clients

"In this book, Jen Burrows and her colleagues identify, expose, and remove the fears that block us not only from successful public speaking but also provide tools that can be used in any situation and at any time. As a writer-producer in Hollywood, I never know when I'm going to be pitching a project or myself; it could be in line at the market or in the office of a studio president. In either situation, Jen's advice is the key to the door of opportunity and I'm glad to have it in my pocket."

Mark Haynes, Writer and Producer, Ironbird Entertainment

"Although focused primarily on professional presentations that include public speaking, this book is ideal for the Business Leader or Manager who needs to verbalize their vision to the workforce. If you have to stand up and deliver an oral presentation of any sort then you MUST read this book because it will help you with the important task of communicating more confidently in general. It teaches all the important lessons on gaining rapport with your audience — and is well structured and easily readable. It's jam-packed with interesting observations, insights and suggestions for improving the way you deliver your message to anyone who needs to hear it!"

Dean Evans, Founder & Principal, Leading Minds Australia

PICTURE THEM NAKED

Everything you ever wanted to know about
presenting and public speaking and were afraid to ask.

JENNIFER BURROWS

Practical, proven and positive techniques
from experts who live their life on the stage.

Picture Them Naked: Everything You Ever Wanted to Know about Presenting and Public Speaking and Were Afraid to Ask.

Editing by Felicity Van Rysbergen (www.wellversed.com.au)
Cover Design by Chameleon Print Design (www.chameleondesign.com.au)
Layout and Typesetting by Chameleon Print Design (www.chameleondesign.com.au)

The moral right of Jennifer Burrows to be identified as the author of this work has been asserted in accordance with the Copyright Designs and Patents Act of 1988.

Published by: McQuarrie House Publishing
Copyright © Jennifer Burrows 2014
First Edition, 2014

All rights reserved. No part of this book may be reproduced or transmitted in any form or by any means, electronic or mechanical, including photocopying, recording or by any information storage and retrieval system, without the written permission of the publisher except for the inclusion of brief quotations in a review.
Published in Australia

ISBN 978-0-9924598-4-0

Disclaimer
All of the information, concepts, skills, techniques and advice contained within this publication are of general comment only and not in any way recommended as individual advice. The intent is to provide a variety of information and a wider range of choices now and in the future, recognising that we all have widely diverse circumstances and viewpoints. While all attempts have been made to verify information provided in this publication, neither the author nor the publisher nor the marketing agents assumes any responsibility for errors, omissions or contrary interpretation of the subject matter whatsoever under any condition or circumstances. Should any reader choose to make use of the information contained herein, this is their decision. It is recommended that the reader obtain their own independent advice and where medical matters are involved, they should firstly consult with their relevant medical practitioner prior to embarking on any information contained within this book.

Where client stories have been used, some names have been changed to protect client privacy.

For
Cameron and Brodie
who were there in the beginning
and
Stephen
who will be there till the end.

The human brain starts working the moment you are born and never stops until you stand up to speak in public.
George Jessel

CONTENTS

Acknowledgements xi
Introduction xiii

Hanging off a Ledge By Your Fingernails
Jennifer Burrows 1

The greatest sense of achievement
Aileen Alegado 25

Find a stage. Promote your success
Danny Davis 35

99% back down when the going gets tough
Fiona Craig 45

Be genuine with your audience and win every time
Julie-Anne Black 55

Don't be a speaker to "be someone." Be a speaker to "do something."
Jesper Jurcenoks 69

Feedback is the breakfast of champions
Karen Ostenried 77

Humour is great for business
Kate Burr 91

You're already a speaker
Kristy Moore 103

It takes confidence in yourself
Lara Shannon 115

The only way to be a speaker is to speak
Leigh-Chantelle 123

Just do what you love
Lisa Page 131

Focus on your audience
Maureen Bell 149

Know exactly where you're going
Mireille Ryan 161

Challenge boundaries and push the envelope
Narelle Lee 171

Take Massive Action Now
Pat Rae 185

A true speaker lives what they talk about
Paul Barrs 203

Don't try to be anyone else
Trish Springsteen 215

Resources

The Ultimate Elevator Pitch 229
The 5 Minute Phobia Cure 233
Preparing Your Speakers Kit 237
Claiming Your Free Bonus Gifts 241
About the Contributors 245

ACKNOWLEDGEMENTS

No book is ever the undertaking of a single individual and this book is no exception. I am profoundly grateful for and deeply indebted to the following people (and dog) who made this book possible:

To the 17 intrepid contributors who put their faith in me to deliver their message, my heartfelt thanks for being part of my vision.

Faye Lanyon for keeping me supplied with endless amounts of chocolate, good humour and gossip. I can't begin to tell you how much I appreciate you.

Karen Russell for not asking questions when I demanded stories of all things that were wonderful in her life on the days when it felt things sucked in mine.

Huge thanks to Natalia Isaacs who showed absolute faith in this project by buying the book before it was finished. And an extra special thank you to Graeme for indulging her love of shopping.

Stephen, Kirsten, Cameron, Kiera and Brodie, thank you for all your love and support. You make it all worthwhile.

A special mention to Dr Roger Callahan the founder of Thought Field Therapy and the creator of the Five Minute Phobia Cure. The world is a poorer place since the passing of Dr Callahan in November 2013. The Five Minute Phobia Cure (p233) is reprinted here with the generous permission of his wife Joanne, the current President and CEO of Callahan Techniques, Ltd. To further explore (and benefit from) Dr Callahan's work please visit www.rogercallahan.com

Luke Harris of Chameleon Designs for comprehending the vision in my head and bringing the cover to life.

Our editor extraordinaire Felicity Van Rysbergen, thank you for cheerfully reading this manuscript for what seems like a thousand times. Your attention to detail leaves me awestruck.

My eternal gratitude to Ramona Lever for incredible headshots of which my favourite appears on the back cover of this book. Your warmth, laughter and amazing talent changed me from a reluctant subject to a raving fan.

To everyone who provided feedback on everything from cover to cover, too many of you to mention but you all know who you are. Thank you.

And Geordie. Whilst no animals were harmed in the writing of this book, Geordie did have his paws walked off and his fur is a little less furry from being patted so often. Thanks for sitting under my desk and keeping me company.

INTRODUCTION

The first time I was called upon to present in a professional capacity was to a large group of people on, horror of horrors, financial services information, which in the hands of an inept presenter can be intensely dull. My terror at such an undertaking must have been immediately obvious as my employer clapped me on the shoulder and said sagely: "Just picture them naked and you'll be fine."

The image of this group in all their naked glory is a picture that will haunt my nightmares until the end of time. Fine was the last thing I was. And, oh boy, was I dull.

I stood at the front of the room, eyes lowered, reading from cards, shaking, my legs tightly crossed protecting who only knows what, biting back tears and all the while fighting the huge lump in my throat that was threatening to choke me. I was torn between the urge to throw up and the desire to put the back of my hand to my sweaty brow, breathily whisper "oh, my" and delicately swoon to the floor.

Except...

With no *coup de grace* in sight I pushed on to the bitter end — much to the sorrow of my audience whom I'm sure wanted to be anywhere except watching me die a slow, torturous, possibly career terminating death.

It was, without doubt, one of the most traumatising events of my life. Presenting, public speaking, putting myself on display — whatever you like to call it — was very definitely not for me. I decided I was never going to do it again. Yet, despite trying valiantly to escape presentation hell, my then employer had different ideas, and so did every employer that followed.

Unfortunately the ability to present is a sought-after skill, highly valued in business. Many companies today include a verbal presentation as part of their standard recruitment procedure and as a component of their internal promotion process. Being able to confidently, concisely and clearly articulate your ideas, business recommendations and, indeed, the business itself is part and parcel of the success package.

And for entrepreneurs, business owners, business development managers and others in sales-focussed roles, success lives and dies on the ability to communicate their offering to a group of strangers, sometimes with little time to prepare.

A highly sought-after skill, a top requirement for success in business, a skill upon which your career lives and dies… and yet presenting and public speaking is considered to be the one thing people fear more than death.

Fear of public speaking is a genuine phobia — it's called glossophobia. What a marvellous word. Actually, it's the first part of the word I'm really taken with. Associated words pop into my head, such as 'shiny' and 'lustrous.' But how do these words fit with phobia? Let's check in with my old friend Dictionary.com. And there it is. Not only are shiny and lustrous definitions of gloss — a secondary definition is also provided:

> *Gloss: a false or deceptively good appearance.*

So a fear of public speaking is technically a false phobia and yet it's more feared than death. As Jerry Seinfeld so eloquently put it: "Most people at a *funeral* would *rather be in the coffin* than *delivering the eulogy.*"

The National Institute of Mental Health (NIMH), in addition to providing me with that marvellous word glossophobia, further defines a fear of public speaking as speech anxiety. Hmm, does that mean fear of public speaking is an anxiety disorder? And, if so, isn't that a condition you can be medicated for? Now I'm really curious. Put your hand up if you take Xanax for public speaking… go on, no judgement here.

It's so easy to say fear of public speaking is a false phobia, expect you to move past it and — yippy-ki-yay — you're a superior speaker brimming with self-confidence and not a shaky hand or bead of sweat in sight. Me personally? My speciality is (metaphorically speaking), hanging off a ledge by my fingernails.

And I'm not alone. There's a further 17 professional speakers in this book who will also tell you they suffer from nerves to some degree. Which means YOU are not alone either. In fact, you're in very good company.

In their 2013 research, the NIMH noted 74% of people suffer from speech anxiety. That's huge. And it doesn't gender discriminate. Male sufferers number 73%, female 75%.

I've run hundreds of presentation skills workshops, worked with thousands of participants and, while managing nerves is a huge component of achieving success as a speaker, it's not the be all and end all. Confidence in front of a crowd will only take you so far.

In the pages ahead you'll hear 18 outstanding accounts from real and accessible people who live their life on the stage. Each has put business competitiveness aside to share their hard-won wisdom with you. Each has carefully written their responses to provide you with great content, valuable insights and the highs or — oh, yes — lows of their careers.

Whether you want to be a professional speaker, more clearly able to articulate your business offerings, present more confidently at work or even just be more assured in your next impromptu speech, then 'Picture Them Naked, everything you ever wanted to know about presenting and public speaking and were afraid to ask' is the right book for you.

In addition to the insights of 18 professional speakers the book includes a number of useful resources:

- The five-minute phobia cure for busting nerves for good

- A speakers kit template for those wanting to speak professionally and get paid for it

- Elevator pitch examples and an easy-to-follow format for preparing your own.

You'll find tips to constructing a great presentation, how professionals prepare for an event, pre-speech rituals, advice for getting started in speaking, loads of wisdom on everything from how they think to their greatest successes and, somewhat entertainingly, their biggest disasters. This is your chance to pick the brains of 18 professionals all in one place.

Plus, a number of contributors have generously offered gifts to every reader, all of which will add value to your speaking career, future presentations, business and life in general. You can find them all at **www.picturethemnakedbook.com.au**

As you read through this book, whether you devour it from start to finish or jump to whichever chapter interests you, make note of the wise advice given by those who do speak for a living or who also, like me, teach others how to get the best out of themselves as presenters and speakers. We've made the mistakes so you won't have to. You'll still make mistakes, just hopefully not the ones we have.

Last but not least… reading this book is a great start. But acting on what you've read will determine its real value to you. As you practice what we've preached, please let us know of your successes — we'd love to celebrate with you.

Jennifer Burrows

Phone: +61 3 9017 1843
Email: jburrows@valueforlife.com.au
Website: www.valueforlife.com.au
or   www.jenniferburrows.com

Jennifer Burrows

Hanging Off a Ledge by your Fingernails

Born and raised in Scotland, Jennifer delivered her first presentation at the ripe old age of eight motivating her similarly aged 'sales force' to sell painted stones to the neighbours. This was also her first entrepreneurial venture and did a roaring trade until her mum found out.

Recognising an overwhelming need for an overhaul in corporate communications, Jen began the process of transforming the lacklustre to the remarkable. Touting the philosophy that the best presenters and communicators are those who are natural and themselves when communicating with others, her mission is to maximise the ability to persuade and influence while significantly increasing the confidence, authority and presence of those presenting to a diverse range of audiences.

Since 2005, she has advised organisations on their internal and external communications, facilitating transformational training events and assessing, and deconstructing thousands of corporate pitches and presentations.

Jen's genuine interest in the development of human potential through coaching and mentoring, coupled with her professional experience means she has an intimate understanding of both the interpersonal demands placed on today's senior leaders and the know-how to cultivate an individual's promise in presentation and communication skills.

As a professional speaker on the business and motivational circuit, Jen is sought after for her insights and anecdotes. Her significant experience ensures her delivery is as informed as it is entertaining.

Jen currently lives in Melbourne, Australia, is married to the most wonderful (and more significantly, the most understanding) man on earth, has four children, a free spirited 'bit of everything' dog and is passionately involved with a number of charitable organisations.

Do you suffer from nerves and if so how do you manage them?

I'd love to say that after all this time and the amount of pitches, presentations and speeches I've been involved in that I had no nerves. But that would be less than true.

There are days when I'm seriously hanging off a ledge by my fingernails. This happened to me only recently. I was about to deliver a 5-hour long presentation to a group of CEOs. There were no small potatoes in that room. And that's what I kept saying to myself. Over and over again I told myself stories about this audience and what they would think of me.

And I actually talked myself out of my usual speaking elan.

For me, what's most strange is that I get great results from nerves. I've worked with thousands of people — one-on-one and in groups — and I equip them with all the tools to succeed beyond their wildest dreams. You'd think, armed with all this knowledge, that I'd find it easier, that I'd be able to deal with speaking with more aplomb.

Yet, I think that's why clients respond to me so well. I still get nervous, so I genuinely understand where they're at when they come to me. I feel their pain — the sweat running down their necks, the trembling voice, when they're throwing up in the waste basket and their hands are shaking so badly they can't hold a pen. I feel the pain and I remember what it was like for me in the early days.

My nerves are now significantly different to what they were 15 or even 10 years ago. Nowadays they only pop up prior to a presentation and, although they don't feel great, I do recognise them for what they really are — my desire to do well and the fact I care about my audience extracting maximum value from the time they spend in a room with me.

Truthfully, the day I go on stage with no nerves at all is the day I'll quit. Because I'll know I've stopped giving a damn.

How do I manage them? Great question — there's a lot to the answer, so hang on to your hat. Actually, scrap that. Most people don't have time to do everything so these are the things I do when I've jumped off the public speaking ledge and I'm hanging by my fingernails:

My top seven non-negotiables to manage nerves.

1. Start by acknowledging you know your stuff. You wouldn't be speaking on it if you didn't. This is the biggie for me — I'm not so worried that the audience won't like me or my presentation. But I do suddenly become quite convinced I've no idea what I'm talking about. I knew it seven ways to Sunday yesterday — but that was yesterday, and today I know nothing. Even as I'm sharing this with you, I'm laughing at myself and my own innate ability to be absolutely ridiculous.

2. Make yourself relax by doing some simple vocal exercises to help warm up your voice. Start by breathing deeply into the bottom part of your lungs (you should feel your rib cage expanding slightly higher than your navel). Stretch your arms towards the ceiling as you breathe in. Then sigh loudly as you drop your arms and your body forward with a *woomph* sound.

   Sighing is your signal to your body that everything's okay, everything's just perfect as it is and it's time to relax. Repeat this over and over again — if you can do it for a full minute you'll really notice the difference (I use this for more than just speaking; it's a fantastic stress releaser — a hundred *woomphs* and I feel amazing).

3. If you're somewhere where you won't be told to be quiet, make a siren sound (like a fire engine or ambulance), starting from a high note to a lower note at the bottom part of your vocal range. With enough practice, you should be able to find the low note connect-

ing to the place located right above the navel. This is your natural vocal pitch. This is also fun!

4. A real non-negotiable is to prepare a crackerjack introduction. The stronger the introduction the better off you'll be. Think of it like a rocketship taking off for the moon — the biggest thrust is at the beginning as it gains the momentum needed to push off the ground. Once the rocket exits the atmosphere, it's a smooth ride.

    Start your presentation in a way that works for you. I really need audience feedback upfront, (don't judge me ☺ ... it's part of my need to be liked). Once I feel that the audience and I have connected there's nothing that can stop me, no question can knock me off my perch, no technological hiccups can throw me. I become unstoppable because I can feel the audience driving me on to succeed, which leads me on to tip 5.

5. Your audience desperately wants you to be good. How many times have you sat in a presentation willing the presenter on to great things because you don't want to be bored senseless or squirming in embarrassment as they stumble from point to point offering excuses and apologies? Accept that the audience wants you to succeed and *woomph* a couple of times more.

6. CYA (also known as Cover Your Anatomy). Ensure you know your equipment inside out — leave nothing to chance when it comes to technology. *Always, always, always* take your own laptop to an event. Have your presentation backed up to an external drive as a contingency — if the organisers already have a laptop set up you can then simply plug in your external device. If they haven't got a laptop available and have overlooked telling you this, then you're prepared (this happened to me recently, which was one of the reasons I was hanging off a ledge by my fingernails).

    If you're using powerpoint, know your slide order. And ensure you have a copy of your notes on a table nearby should you need to refer to them. Note that they belong on the table and NEVER in your hands.

CYA also means rehearsal. You should have rehearsed your presentation (out loud) umpteen times before you go on. There's a reason for this — the more you rehearse, the more familiar you are with your presentation. When you rehearse out loud your mouth develops a muscle memory that will help you if you run into trouble (this advice is in direct contradiction of my mother, who always told me my mouth would get me into trouble. Well, from where I'm standing now, rehearse out loud consistently and your mouth will get you OUT of trouble).

7. Always carry a printed copy of your notes. As experienced presenters we can become a little complacent and rely less on notes (although seriously you should never rely on notes, it's very bad form). Trust me on this, the day you have no notes will be the day you need them (as an example, see my answer to the question about the worst things that have happened to me during a presentation).

How do you prepare for a presentation? Do you have a specific method you follow?

I follow a specific method, which is also the one I teach. I outline my presentation first using four steps:

1. **Create a final message.** You always want the audience to walk away remembering your presentation. Get this message down to 25 words. There's no magic to the 25-word maximum, except that you can usually remember that much and you can say it without running out of breath.

2. **Brainstorm an agenda** or 3-5 high-level chunks of information you intend to cover. Keep this really high level and innocuous — the last thing you want is questions at this point.

3. **Ensure your agenda items support your final message** by establishing one key take-away per agenda item. If your audience remembers nothing else except this point, your whole argument will still hang together. Keep the key take-away short and to the

point — ideally 5-7 words. Does it support your final message? If yes, you are on the right track. If no, then either the agenda item is too low level (and is possibly the key take-away) or you have the wrong agenda heading.

4. **Give proof.** With the aforementioned in place, now you can select the proof to support your argument (the content of your actual presentation, case studies, facts, figures, anecdotal evidence, etc.). Jot these down as bullet points only. As an aside, the more stories you have the better. Facts tell but stories sell!

Facts tell but stories sell!

Once I have the structure in place, sometimes — not all the time, but sometimes — I write the whole presentation out exactly as I would say it. One of the things you may already have picked up from reading this is that I sound as if I'm speaking rather than writing. That's because I write exactly as I speak. I tend to do this more so when the subject matter is unfamiliar to me. I then rehearse it out loud, starting from the prepared script and whittling it down until I get to a few points no more than a single A4 page. A couple of words per point should be enough to jog your memory and keep you going in the right direction. Remember, Facts Tell... Stories Sell.

Do you have a 'best move'?

There's an exercise I like to do with an audience that — without exception — gets a laugh and reduces audience anxiety (yes, they're anxious, because at this point they have no idea if you're a terrifically engaging speaker or intend to put them to sleep). It also has the added benefit of connecting me to the audience so my need to be liked is met. This exercise is incredibly simple but it gets the audience engaged with me *and* with each other. It's the most basic of all personality profiling tools and can easily be done with any sized audience.

The other side benefit of this exercise is that I learn more about the audience by the way they complete the test. For example:

- Those laughing, chatting and comparing notes are generally the extoverts who will be my allies as I start my presentation. Blessed with a similar need to be liked, they will want the presenter's attention. In presentation land we often refer to these joyful souls as 'easy lays,' for no other reason than they like to engage... with everyone.

- Other audience members will ask me very specific questions around the exercise. I know these are the people who will want all my main points qualified, so giving them additional details now will pay off.

The smart presenter will begin their presentation looking directly at one of the 'easy lays' — rapport with them is easy to achieve and, best of all, these people are so likable that others will follow their lead by engaging.

It works every time, no exceptions.

What are your pre-presentation rituals?

Some may call them superstitions, however I prefer to call these my pre-presentation rituals. I try to make things as easy for myself as possible. That means the less I have to think about on presentation day the better.

I always wear the same outfit on the first day of a 2-day workshop or to a presentation, which to me counts as day one. This outfit has been planned right down to the shoes, the jewellery, the make-up, etc., and I do not deviate from what I've planned. On presentation day you don't want to be concerned with whether you are having a 'fat' day, a 'short' day or plain old indecisiveness about what looks better on you. Plan in advance and stick to the plan.

Always have a contingency outfit prepared. I buy my presentation clothes in sets of two. Yes, I know I'm a little over the top! That's why my bio mentions a significantly understanding husband. Forget about my weirdness and just put the contingency outfit in place. Trust me, you'll thank me one day.

I get out of bed 90 minutes before I normally would to make sure I've drunk coffee, eaten breakfast, reviewed my presentation and have still allowed sufficient time to get there early. This has the additional benefit that if I spill something on myself I have time to change into my contingency outfit. You'd think I'd learn to eat before dressing but no, that would mess up the ritual. I do this regardless of what time the presentation is scheduled for.

Wear flat shoes or runners to get to your presentation and change into heels (if you're a woman or just that way inclined), when you get there. Your feet will thank you and you'll have more energy throughout your presentation.

Under no circumstances do I have my hair cut or coloured the day prior to an event. That's inviting trouble. Enough said, the ladies will know what I mean.

Lastly, there are two songs I sing along with on my way to every event. I enjoy driving to events where I can pump up the volume and really get into it. The songs I listen to? Number one is The Eagles' *Take It To The Limit*. My favourite version is by Vika Bull, which hasn't been around very long (if you haven't heard it yet, I highly recommend. It's unbelieveable). Her voice is a force to be reckoned with and that is exactly how I feel when I sing along. The other is Nina Simone's *Feeling Good*, which really settles me and fills me with happiness.

Find what music pumps you up and what calms you down. Use both effectively.

Did you always know the career path you wanted to take? If not, where did you start from and how did you make the change?

When I was in high school, my reports cards were consistent in one remark: "Jennifer talks too much." In fact, when I attended my 25-year reunion, I encountered one of the teachers who had been very critical of my tendency to verbalise pretty much everything. He told me I had been one of the most vocal students he'd ever had. I waited patiently for the question I knew was coming. It didn't take long.

> "So what do you do for a living?" He asked.

> "I speak," I said. "I speak and I've become an authority on speaking. I also teach speaking, the how-to of constructing and delivering powerful, persuasive and influential arguments that get incredible results. If you can't language a thing, you can't have it. It's that simple."

It was a very satisfying moment.

Although I was a talker in school, the primary reason was to seek attention. I had a desperate need to be accepted and liked, all the while being absolutely terrified that I would be found out as not being good enough for either of those things. I didn't set out to speak for a living or to help others to develop their speaking skills. To be honest, I had no idea you could be paid for that. Even now I'm sure my parents don't think I have a 'real' job.

As the years passed, my wanting to be liked and accepted grew. And so did my fear of being found out. It got to the point where I was petrified of speaking in public, to the extent that if there were more than one person in the room, I would fall completely to pieces. I'm thinking here of a specific tender presentation that I wish I could permanently erase from my memory.

In the midst of completely falling to pieces I'd lose my ability to clearly articulate my ideas. My heart rate would increase — I felt it would pound right through my chest wall. I'd break out in a sweat and droplets would roll down my face and neck, nausea would kick in and my voice would get this warble. I sounded as if I was on the verge of bursting into tears, which, by the way, I was.

Regardless of all of these things, I would still show up to make my monthly report to the board (after all my attempts to bail had been thwarted). I'd be armed to the gills with reports in the vain hope they'd be too busy reading my paperwork to listen or look at me. Unfortunately, there were usually questions and my fear was at such a level that my responses would sound aggressive as I valiantly attempted to maintain a semblance of self-control.

During one of these board reports, one of the Directors (I should point out this company is an enormous international organisation) interjected with a question.

> "Graham, you know, you'll have your turn, but right now I'm speaking — so I'm just going to finish what I'm saying here and then you're welcome to share any comments," I said, rudely.

It was an offensive stance and believe me when I say he took offence.

The CEO took me aside and told me I really needed to get some help to keep my nerves under control or my career was going to be seriously limited. I went through so many presentation skills courses and nothing really helped. I even went to the US to learn — that helped a bit.

Eventually I put together all the bits that I felt worked, added that to a ton of research I'd completed on why people do what they do, added behavioural analysis and understanding and, there it was — a program that worked — and not just for me but for every person I've worked with.

From thereon in I took every opportunity to get on my feet and talk. One of the best things I learned along the way was also the very first thing I spoke on — the Five Minute Phobia Cure developed by Dr. Roger Callahan (more on this later).

Given the topic I figured the least I could do was do it on myself first. I did it twice then went off to the gig. It went better than expected and, although I felt the fear come up inside me, it was as if it was a ball in a pinball machine. I could feel this fear ball bouncing along inside me but not getting traction. There was nothing for it to hold on to; it was the strangest feeling.

It was somewhere along this road that it suddenly occurred to me that if I felt this way it was highly likely that others did too. So, I made the switch, first to a training company prepared to give me a go as a presentation skills trainer. Then I went out on my own with a suite of programs designed to help people achieve everything they wanted. As I said before, if you can't language a thing, you can't have it. My own experiences laid the foundations for me to build a business dedicated to making sure anyone who came across my path would be transformed overnight into the confident speaker they had always wanted to be.

 If you can't language a thing, you can't have it. It's that simple.

What has been one of the biggest challenges you have had to face in business and how did you overcome it?

Isolation would be the biggest hurdle to overcome, followed closely by procrastination. To be brutally honest, though, isolation was the killer for me. Speaking for a living means you tend to work alone — no water cooler conversations, no one stopping by your desk for a chat. If this is something you're used to it can be a little confronting to suddenly be surrounded by four walls and no bodies.

For the first five years, I was pretty fine with it. The biggest challenge became not the four walls but stopping my retired parents from visiting every day (to them being at work meant 7am to 4.30pm, not being at home behind a computer). To this day, I think if you asked them what I do for a living they'd be hard-pressed to answer. Ask my children and they'll tell you, "Oh, mum talks and people listen," a refreshing concept since no one listens when you ask them to pick up their socks or unpack the dishwasher.

Which brings me nicely to the art of procrastination and — oh boy — am I an expert at this.

Whenever I'm preparing for a presentation that is particularly challenging to the point of being a tad unnerving, the most amazing thing happens to me; my body is possessed by an alien being who is obsessed with home-based tasks.

Suddenly the front door needs repainting, the beds stripped and remade, dishwasher emptying, dog walking, wardrobes cleaning out, grocery shopping, weeks meals need planning, I need to get the slow cooker on... you get the picture. I knew I had a real problem when I called a glazier to replace the glass in the windows.

So what did I do? I moved out of home and into business premises. This solved the isolation issue since I was sharing a building with others (woohoo! shared kitchen facilites), but now I had a whole new place to procrastinate over — really how important is it that my office is set up to feng shui perfection? Well that depends on what presentation I'm gearing up for.

Is there a significant quote or saying that you live by?

There are two quotes I keep on the wall of my office. Both are comments I made during presentations:

1. Never underestimate the power of someone lacking in talent who is possessed of great drive, ambition and above all courage. Talent and success are not necessarily synonymous.

2. You've climbed bigger mountains than this.

The first reminds me that I've worked hard to become talented and the second, well it speaks for itself really. Each time I think something's too tough, it's a reminder that this is just a molehill, it's never as bad as the story I'm making up about it.

If you could give just one piece of advice about speaking that would make the biggest difference in one persons life, what would that be?

Show up!

No-one becomes a great speaker overnight, it takes practice; be prepared to pay the price to get a great result. This translates to: do the hours of preparation, do the hours of rehearsal, do the hours of gigs. Do the hours, do the hours, do the hours. There will be mistakes along the way that will be key to your future success — believe me when I say you'll learn significantly more from any mistakes you make than you ever will from gigs that end in rapturous applause. Embrace your mistakes.

 No-one becomes a great speaker overnight, it takes practice; be prepared to pay the price to get a great result.

Absolutely critical is the way in which you review your own performance. Rather than beating yourself up for what didn't work, what can you learn from it?

Example:

You've asked the audience a question at the beginning and no one responded. What will you do differently next time?

The truth is audiences are sheeple, they need to be led — so how can you lead them? Maybe you could ask a question requiring a yes response, raise your own hand, nod at the audience and say 'yes' pausing strategically along the way. Then follow up with another yes response question, do the same thing and watch them begin to follow you. Then do it again.

There is an added benefit to this tactic. Let me put this to you — how good is it that you have an audience saying yes to you and you haven't told them anything yet?

Hmmm... something to think about!

What is the first step that someone could take if they decided to follow in your footsteps today?

First things first. Get your house in order. And by that I mean create a speaker's kit for yourself.

Your speaker's kit should have a short biography of who you are and a list of topics you can speak on with a short blurb about each. Creating my own first speaker's kit was more than a little unnerving so, on the off chance you feel the same way, I've included a template that you can use freely until the end of time (or until you develop something even better, which of course I hope you'll share with me). See page 233.

I know the question was, what is the first thing, but here are a few other things that may prove helpful:

- Identify groups that may find you appealing as a speaker and market yourself to them. Send them a copy of your speaker's kit and offer your services. Be prepared to not get paid for speaking, however ensure you have something to sell at the end of your presentation, such as a book, CD, program, service, or at the very least ask them to visit your website and subscribe to your newsletter in exchange for a free report on xyz (that way you can market to them later).

- If this is too much for you at the get go, ensure you bring with you a great book (such as this one ☺) that you can give away as a gift from a business card draw. By encouraging everyone to put their business cards in a bowl you have secured their details for later marketing, and it will be warm marketing since they've already been exposed to you. Who do you already know that may belong to groups or organisations who may be interested in you as a speaker? Ask them to help you out. You'll be surprised at how many people will be happy to lend a hand.

- Attend industry events (not necessarily your own industry), and make contacts that may become referrals that may become speaking gigs. One of the best gigs I ever got was through attending an industry event that wasn't remotely connected to me — I just thought the speakers might be worth listening to (note: there were speakers, which means they use speakers) and I may make some valuable contacts.

- At the after-event drinks a gorgeous woman walked past me wearing the most amazing shoes. I complimented her on them (admittedly a woman admiring another woman's shoes is usually a great conversation starter, guys may need something altogether different). This became a discussion on decent places to buy great shoes. I had no agenda other than to enjoy the conversation and as a shoe lover my interest was genuine. As things turned out, the woman was a senior leader in the organisation that was hosting the event. Four months later I was their featured speaker.

- Who do you know who could refer you to someone they know? Review your contact list and ensure you continually add to it.

- Above all, be prepared to answer clearly and concisely when someone asks you what you do. This means having your elevator pitch ready. You don't have an elevator pitch yet? Not a problem, see page 229 for the steps to putting one together.

How did you get your first gig, who was it with and what was the experience like?

I'd run a workshop for a group that had been highly successful. Some months later they called me and said not only had they learned a lot about the subject matter but they'd learned a lot about themselves. The feeling was that I could add a lot of value to their upcoming seminar — would I be a guest speaker. This would be my first 'real' gig and they wanted to pay me $350. It was astonishing to me that it was possible to get paid for standing and speaking about something you were passionate about.

I put extraordinary effort into preparing for this presentation. If these people were willing to pay me then I was going to give them all that I had to make it a wonderful experience for them.

By the time the presentation was ready I was thrilled with it. I'd rehearsed my timings, and it had a crackerjack opening that involved audience participation. There was nothing I hadn't accounted for and therein was my first lesson. You cannot account for absolutely everything.

I hadn't been able to get into the auditorium ahead of time so I was flying blind from the perspective of familiarity with my surroundings. As it turns out, it was a university lecture theatre and the stage was HUGE, the biggest I'd ever seen. The only thing on it would be little old me.

The entire presentation went out of my head to be replaced by comedian Billy Connelly's performance where he had huge screens set up around the stage that would instantly transform into pictures (with sound effects) of a clapping cheering audience every time he raised his arms. What was great was him telling his human audience that, if they sucked, he was bringing in these guys; cue turn to blank screens and a cheering audience. I giggled to myself... so got to get me one of those. And I'm back in the zone, no problem.

This was also the first time I'd seen the run sheet. I already knew I was the speaker standing between this audience and lunch. What I hadn't known was that I was following a very serious presentation by a learned professor on the subject of 'Sudden Infant Death Syndrome.' Then I read the rest of the run sheet — it was all serious stuff. And I was there to deliver a motivational speech on the pursuit of happiness. It was possible I had my work cut out for me.

It started badly. I was standing on the edge of the stage, fully miked up so I couldn't mutter to myself, facing a full auditorium and unable to recall my opening lines. Of course, I'd chosen to quote from the work of the amazing Marianne Williamson. I looked at the audience and they looked back. I took a deep breath, rearranged my features into a puzzled frown and walked what felt like a million miles to the farside of the stage where the lectern and my notes were. I picked up my bottle of water and drank. As I put it back down I looked at my notes, read the opening line and felt my brain swell as memory returned. Turning on my heel, I marched to the middle of the stage, then to the front and began.

Everything went like clockwork from that point on. I was having fun and the audience were almost fully engaged. I say almost because there was one woman in the front row to my far left, last seat in the row, who appeared unengaged. I did give it a go and when that proved unsuccessful I figured that whatever was going on was about her and not me. I chose to refocus my energy on the 99.99% of the audience who seemed to be thoroughly enjoying themselves.

Then came THE question and my next lesson.

A question will appear, at times, that you could not have predicted. In my case the question was: "How do you manage children in the supermarket?" Remember my subject was the pursuit of happiness. Obviously managing children in the supermarket was fundamental to this woman's happiness. So I figured I'd give it a shot.

I explained I had no answer that would work 100% of the time for 100% of children, but if it would be helpful I'd be glad to share what I did with my children. Standing in the middle of the stage I sang loudly and unaccompanied Janis Joplin's, *Oh Lord Won't You Buy Me A Mercedes Benz*. This is what *I* do and it works for me every time, no exceptions. When I begin to sing my children run in one direction and I continue shopping. On very good days other shoppers will join in.

All these years later I still look back on that presentation as one of the most wonderful experiences of my life. It set the benchmark for me as well.

Key lessons arising from my first gig:

1. It was nothing like I thought it would be.

2. Not everyone will be interested so focus on those who are.

3. Always have your notes nearby.

4. Being miked up means you can be heard but also means you can't talk yourself down off the ledge, at least not out loud.

5. Not everything will go according to plan, so be flexible.

6. Get a copy of the run sheet in advance.

7. You'll probably get a question you can't predict.

Did you ever want to 'give up' because it all got a bit too much?

Only on the bad days! Let me count the meltdowns. I shared this question with my husband who laughed uproariously and suggested perhaps he was better placed to answer it. Apparently, my meltdowns are not something I keep to myself — and here was I thinking I'd been wildly successful at keeping a stiff upper lip.

My advice to you: have your meltdown, let out all the frustration, fear, angst and whatever else is going on, let it out and let it out loud. BUT…

Set a timer for however many minutes you need. Wallow until you are all wallowed out (my personal favourite is to roll up a towel and beat on a chair whilst screaming. It's exhausting *and* burns calories). When the timer sounds, move on, it's done. Get your butt off the floor and do whatever it is that you have to do.

What can people do to stay on track, especially when times get tough?

There will be times when things get tough, I kid you not. There will be days when you're hanging off a ledge by your fingernails, days when it's all too much and days when you just-plain-old-want-to-quit.

Most advice will tell you to push through. But how can you when you feel so low you don't think you have the strength to stand up, let alone push though with any degree of force?

Two things I know that work:

1. **Do something nice for someone else.** The only condition is that it must involve you leaving your desk. Go send a card, buy a gift, take flowers to someone you know who could use a pick me up (not yourself), help load a container headed to East Timor, take some tinned goods to a charity. There's always someone doing it tougher than you, so make his or her day a little easier. Better yet, do it anonymously.

2. **Regardless of weather,** go for a walk for a minimum of 40 minutes. Think only of all that is good in your world. Make a mental list of all you have to be grateful for.

Both will help you step outside the 'tough' zone, re-energise you, refocus your thoughts on the bigger picture and, above all, calm you down so you can start again.

What is the worst thing that has ever happened to you during a speaking engagement and how did you recover your equilibrium to continue?

Oh disasters, let me count the ways... I'm the queen of disasters in speaking. Actually, truth be told, there's probably another book in that. But I digress.

The moment that still makes me squirm is the day my pants fell down.

They didn't fall all the way down, just partially. On ladies' pants there is a button and a zipper. For some reason the zipper had come loose from its moorings and the button had popped off (I found it on the floor later). Fortunately for me, my pants had pockets. Actually all my pants have pockets because, when I'm presenting I like the option of putting one hand in a pocket — it gives an air of informality that is very acceptable to an audience. It also serves to keep my hands under control. (One of the most common questions I'm asked is what do I do with my hands?) With one secured in my pocket and one relaxed at my side I'm less likely to hold hands with myself or use the prayer stance (palms together, fingers pointing towards the ceiling) unconsciously communicating 'please let this be over').

> **The moment that still makes me squirm is the day my pants fell down.**
>
> *So here I am, zipper down, button on the floor and my pants leisurely heading south. Without missing a beat, I put my hand in my pocket, scrunch up the material and hold on for dear life. All the Gods were with me that day — I was wearing a shirt outside my pants that hid what I was doing. What is notable is the room I was in. Had it been all women I would have confessed, laughed it off and ducked behind the whiteboard to dress myself. However, this was an all-male audience and reducing my authority in the room was not an option. So I held on until the end, then went and did my pants up.*

Apart from material possessions, money brings significant opportunity. Can you share with us the opportunity you are most fond or proud of that money has given you?

The best thing about making money is the ability to give it away. I don't want to sound pious or goody two shoes, because I'm not. What I am is grateful.

I'm profoundly blessed and, while it took a long time for me to get to this place, I'm making the most of it. I go to the Salvation Army stores pretty much every month, select a bunch of their secondhand clothes, pay for them then drive to the nearest donation bin and put them in the chute. It's more fun than just donating money. I like to do stuff that makes people feel important and reminds them that they matter in the big scheme of life.

One day I was standing in line. Two women were in front of me wanting to purchase a painting but didn't have enough money and so were attempting unsuccessfully to haggle with the guy at the checkout. I stepped forward and asked him how much the painting was, and what price he would absolutely accept.

The women immediately got in my face quite rudely. It was their painting, they'd seen it first. I smiled gently. "I know it's your painting and I can see how much you want to have it. I'm asking how much it is to make sure I have enough in my wallet to give you as a gift so you can take it home," I told them.

You could have heard a pin drop. The checkout guy suddenly had a best price, which was less than the original asking price. The painting went home with the people to whom it mattered. My smile was so big that day and I was on such a high that I didn't come down for hours. Definitely up there as one of the best experiences of my life.

What makes you stand out from your competitors?

I heard something once along the lines of: those who can, do, and those who can't, teach. From my understanding, most presentation skills coaches teach brilliantly, but they're not on the speaking circuit. And most speakers are not coaching others in how to become outstanding presenters and public speakers.

What this means is that those wanting to become truly great speakers are being educated in theory only as their teachers lack the war stories of either having tanked in front of a live audience or soared the dizzying heights of delivering at the top of your game (and everything in between). This is what sets me apart. I am one of those rare few who does both. When I began coaching in presentation skills I recognised that you can't learn to swim by reading a book and neither can you teach with any degree of authenticity unless you do the do.

The other thing that sets me apart is my presenting and communicating philosophy: the best presenters, the best speakers, are those who are natural and themselves when they speak with an audience.

When I'm working with you, the very first thing I do is assess who you are when you're just being yourself. Once I know that, it's easy to establish if you pull on presentation underpants or take off your natural personality when you present. My objective — other than making you the best speaker you can possibly be — is to ensure you remain true to who you are, because this is something that is sustainable long term.

 The best presenters, the best speakers, are those who are natural and themselves.

Aileen Alegado

Aileen Alegado

The Greatest Sense of Achievement

Dr Aileen Alegado was born in Manila, Philippines in 1980 and her family immigrated to New Zealand in 1993.

After receiving first class honors for her Bachelor of Science, she was accepted into the Clinical Psychology Doctoral Programme at Auckland University in 2003 graduating in 2008 with high distinctions. During her doctorate, she was one 75 students worldwide to receive a scholarship to attend a prestigious summer school at the International Neuropsychological Society.

Aileen opened her own private practice in South Yarra at age 29. She sees psychology for all aspects of life, not just for those suffering from mental health issues. Aileen ran psycho-educational life skills seminars that were highly popular and accessible for everyone. Topics such as — 'Preventing Self Sabotage', 'Managing Stress', 'Stop Over-analyzing', 'Why Perfect Isn't Good Enough' were received well publicly. These seminars have not only furthered her goal in reaching a wider audience but have cemented her skills in public speaking.

As a professional speaker and coach, her natural confidence, presence and ability to relate across demographics have helped her achieve success in her industry. She is the director of Mindset Consulting with two offices in Melbourne, and clinics opening in Sydney in 2014.

What do you believe it takes to be a professional speaker?

Being a good speaker isn't how much you know or how much of an 'expert' you are. It's about how you make your ideas accessible to your audience and still be engaging. A great speaker is attuned to the experience (or process) of his/her audience rather than the 'outcome' of giving the perfect presentation — so being flexible with a good sense of humour helps.

A good speaker is someone who shows passion in what they are speaking about, is genuine and can show enthusiasm. Having qualities such as humility at the same time as being inspirational is often a tough balance to achieve.

Sometimes speakers can have a lot of knowledge but be 'stiff' when presenting information. This can distract people from feeling connected and learning from you or stop them from taking away key messages. I personally believe in seeing a speaker as someone human and letting his or her personality shine through. They will come across more friendly and relaxed and add an element of spontaneity to the presentation. Being able to take feedback on board is also one quality of a presenter that I admire. It's never easy to get up there in front of people, let alone take criticism.

Do you suffer from nerves and if so how do you manage them?

Yes. Public speaking is one of the most commonly experienced phobias. Like most, I have the usual negative thoughts and anxieties around, "Will I know enough," "What if I look stupid," "What if people ask questions I don't know the answers to?" These thoughts would make anyone anxious. So I try to normalise them and make sure I reframe them into a more balanced view that's helpful.

At the end of the day, I know these thoughts are always there despite years of giving successful presentations. To counteract them, I ensure I prepare adequately and try to see public speaking as an opportunity to learn and be inspirational. I try to give back to others as much as I can. I also see it as a privilege to be in a position where people give you their time and attention — and I hold this as something to value rather than being afraid of it.

Physically I also keep healthy to manage stress, so I can genuinely get up in front of people and be energetic for them. I practice mindfulness, meditation and yoga, which all have elements of restoring calm and peace internally. Finding something that relaxes you is an important element of staying positive for any challenge.

How did you build your confidence as a speaker?

I practiced my skills on a regular basis and attended conferences or seminars where I could observe and learn from other great speakers. I constantly asked for honest feedback from participants, and was humble and honest about what I didn't know — so that I could continue to work on those weaknesses.

I think people respect you more if you're not trying to hide behind a facade of being superior. I operate on this level of transparency when I'm speaking — it has always given me positive experiences and extra confidence. I've made myself say 'yes' to speaking opportunities, no matter their size. And of course — Practice, Practice, Practice! Sometimes I make my family and critique my presentation before it goes out for public consumption!

What business are you in and what services does it offer?

I own a boutique private psychology practice based in Melbourne and Sydney. We primarily deliver individual and couples therapy for those struggling with mood issues and life concerns. We also offer psychological services such as life skills seminars for community groups and deliver workshops to help small to medium-sized business to improve staff efficiency using psychology principles for effective change and productivity increase. In addition, I provide clinical supervision and mentoring programmes for other clinicians/psychologists and executive coaching.

Some would say it's a tough business listening to people's problems, but I don't see it that way that at all. I believe I'm in the business of offering solutions and being part of something invaluable. I get a lot of satisfaction from empowering people and guiding them towards positive change.

What do you believe was your biggest sacrifice in letting the business off the ground?

Time and financial security. It's hard to get your name out there. For the first year while I built the practice I worked 6 days for approximately 10 hours per day. There definitely wasn't a lot of time for leisure, exercise or anything else! I didn't resent it though, I was working for myself and I believed this was a short-term sacrifice for a lot more freedom later on. I'm glad I didn't give up.

What have been your highlights in speaking?

Being told I should have my own TV show!

Speaking gives me an avenue to share my knowledge and passion for psychology, and it reinforces principles and values to live by and therefore be a better person. It's allowed me to meet so many people and created opportunities I otherwise wouldn't have.

Those who attend my seminars often recommend me to their friends and family and that's how I've grown my business. I also feel lucky to receive genuine gratitude from my audience — people come up to me to say how inspired and motivated my talks make them feel, which is such an invaluable gift. I've done my job well if people can take home a couple of key messages they didn't know before. Recognition and validation is great, but I know true validation lies in what's unsaid (i.e., shifts in people's actions, thinking and ideas).

What is your approach to marketing and how did you get your name out into the marketplace?

Word of mouth is the best kind of advertising. If you do good work and believe in what you have to offer, people follow! There's a lot to be said for positive energy — it sells itself! I also network regularly and take into account people's needs and feedback to improve aspects of my work or business where I can. I'm genuinely interested in business, in people, and what people are doing — I let it guide me intuitively to what I need to do next. So, even socially, I find myself talking about psychology.

If you had to start over, would you do anything differently?

I would have started everything sooner! In the early days of my career, fear of failure tended to minimise the risks I took. I had very high expectations for myself, which ironically stunted my success.

It's also good to be inspired by others. I now know that no one started off 'perfect' — if I waited until I was good at something, I'd never start anything. I wish I'd believed in myself more in the beginning and had sought mentors from the word go.

 If I waited until I was good at something, I'd never start anything.

Do you recall making a conscious decision to be a speaker? If so, when was it and why?

It wasn't a conscious decision, but I always knew public speaking was an invaluable skill to have. I'm in the business of understanding people. We need to communicate in order to understand each other. Learning strategies to do this more confidently was part and parcel of my professional development.

My presenting experience began with co-facilitating 'group' therapy in the public sector. I received great feedback, which was helpful in reinforcing me to continue. While these therapy sessions were free, it was my job to make sure they found them helpful and came back again.

Over time, I worked on building the confidence and skills to become better at speaking publicly. Paradoxically, more and more opportunities seemed to fall into my lap! I still don't really think of this as a 'job' *per se* — as I talk a lot to people in therapy every day, I just adjust my thinking about speaking roles as doing my day job to a 'bigger audience.'

Did you have to change your mindset surrounding public speaking? If so, how did you do it?

Yes, I used to view public speaking fearfully. I thought I'd be open to scrutiny, which meant that I didn't enjoy it as much. Eventually I changed my mindset and saw it as an opportunity. I also surrounded myself with like-minded people who believed in what I was doing and were genuinely excited for me. I think there's a lot of psychology involved in public speaking, and it certainly comes across to your audience how much you are aware of this.

Most speakers tend to believe what they have to say (content) is what people are there for. I agree, but it's how you say it (process) that makes people remember your message and their experience. So content alone is often not enough.

Most speakers tend to believe what they have to say (content) is what people are there for. I agree, but it's how you say it (process) that makes people remember your message and their experience.

What have you found are the best methods or strategies for keeping motivated and focussed?

Keep focussed by having an overall 'vision.' Ask yourself what you're good at and work on your weaknesses.

I try to set practical and realistic goals first, then break them down into smaller, more achievable parts. Cognitive methods that motivate me include focusing on things that push me forwards and not backwards (i.e. Rewarding myself for hard work, validating myself based on previous achievements, using positive affirmations and creating an environment that supports success). Understand that no one achieved great things by doing easy things. I'm drawn to people who are inspiring and knowledgeable in areas I'm not.

Find out what you love and do more of it. Think in ways that minimise struggle — not every day will be easy but neither will every day be hard. When things fall flat, instead of seeing failure I focus on learning and motivating myself to do better next time.

Is there a significant quote or saying you live by?

Every accomplishment starts with the decision to try. If you wait for the day you're good at something you'll never do anything. And yes, sometimes that means you're NOT actually going to be good at that one thing, but that's OK too, as long as you've tried.

If you could give just one piece of advice about speaking that would make the biggest difference in one person's life, what would that be?

Enjoy the opportunity, be yourself and don't try to be anyone else.

People can usually tell if you're trying too hard. You then lose the connection with your audience. View the privilege to be up there speaking as a form of validation already. You can't please everyone and sometimes you miss the point that you're up there for a good reason!

> *People can usually tell if you're trying too hard. You then lose the connection with your audience.*

Apart from material possessions, money brings significant opportunity. Can you share with us the opportunity you are most fond or proud of that money has given you?

Money gives you the freedom to experience life in a somewhat extraordinary way. Seeing the world is the best thing money can buy. It's the one thing you buy that makes your life richer.

What does success mean to you and how does one achieve it?

Success is different for everyone. For me, success is being free from fear, loving what you do and being driven to do more of it. It doesn't have to be limited to work — it can also be the result of aspects of your life that create value and purpose (i.e. Sharing knowledge, being an inspiration or being inspired).

Success is achieved by deciding to pursue and take responsibility for the steps you need to take to be successful. You won't always get it right; people won't always like you. But you won't get it wrong every time, either. Success is the experience of believing, loving and liking yourself and what you do.

What do you think stops people from achieving the level of success they desire?

Fear — fear of rejection and fear of failure, which perpetuates the lack of confidence to take risks. I see this a lot in counseling. I believe it's the major barrier to success *and* happiness. Being fearful to take risks means you miss out on great opportunities. You'll feel stagnated, de-motivated and lack general vitality for anything! There is an innate desire to avoid things that scare us. We don't want to be vulnerable. Ironically, the things that scare us can also provide the greatest sense of achievement when we overcome them.

 The things that scare us also provide the greatest sense of achievement when we overcome them.

What is the most important piece of advice anyone has ever given you?

My grandfather told me I could do anything if I just believed in myself. Reward hard work, work smarter not harder and practice expressing gratitude every day.

What is the most you have earned at once — i.e. in one transaction, one sale, one speaking engagement?

$800 for 20 minutes.

What keeps you from retiring and lying on the beach every day?

I'd get bored. Lying on a beach makes a great holiday but it's not a life. Don't get me wrong; I love lying on the beach! But life is about feeling challenged and stimulated. I do think it's important to get a balance between experiencing challenges and taking time out for pleasure and relaxation.

Do you buy lottery tickets? Why or why not?

Sometimes. I know the odds but someone always wins, right? Optimism gets the better of me.

Danny Davis

**Find a stage
Promote your success**

Successful entrepreneur, strategist, consultant, mentor and speaker, Danny "The Innovation Coach" will motivate and guide audiences to achieve profitable innovation in their lives and business.

He brings real-world experience from his own successful business leadership and from advising hundreds of client organisations as an innovation coach, commercialisation expert, technology management expert, author of governance frameworks, corporate futurist and Agent of Change.

Danny helps audiences find the keys to innovation, strategy and corporate agility already are in their own hands — and sets them on the journey towards more powerful, effective and more fulfilling working lives.

Danny nurtures and challenges the traditional thinking of small and large corporates, government enterprises and the boards and executives who lead them. His reframing of innovation as a strongly managed portfolio of investments in business improvement helps organisations build their own capacity, frameworks and culture for ongoing successful business innovation.

As one of Australia's leading corporate innovators, Danny contributes through Standards Australia on the development of international it governance standards, is a member of Australian Industry Group's Software and Services Member Reference Group and advises a number of boards. He has been instrumental in founding several successful service companies, and mentors entrepreneurial business owners.

Outside his advisory experience Danny has been co-producer and co-presenter of comedy radio, has worked and performed improvised theatre with Impro Melbourne, was festival director of the recent South Melbourne Street Fair, was awarded the UK computer book of the year award, has written extensively for journals, and is sought after for expert commentary and keynote addresses for conferences and corporate events.

What do you believe are the top 5 attributes of a successful speaker?

- Have something of value for every audience

- Be passionate, genuine and engaging

- Listen to your audience and go with what's working on the day

- Understand that you're there to support the show — don't let your ego get away from you

- Know how to count to five.

What makes for a good gig?

It's important to leave an audience changed. I like to reach in and reshape people's minds. It's one thing to change an audience emotionally or energetically, but it's another thing to rewire them completely.

It's easy enough to rev up an audience and leave them sold on the power of guts and determination. But how many of us continue to identify with the one-legged survivor of a plane crash on the north face of Everest when we get back home to the kids, or see the same desk in the same office the next day? These things don't last.

I've done a good job if I can make people see their world in a different way. I've earned my money if people leave with a different understanding of how their world works, how their organisation functions and how the ideas in their head really fit into the real world.

A fresh outlook allows people to use the tools and skills they already have in fresh ways. I can teach new skills — but like any other presenter, they'll fade if the person in the audience doesn't apply them straight away.

If I can change the way people see the world, well, that will stay with them forever — and will impact how they apply themselves to every new situation.

What kind of training/development did you undertake to become the speaker you are today?

I've got 30 years of professional experience and I've mentored thousands of executives across hundreds of organisations. I kicked off a PhD to provide an evidence base to underpin my methodologies. And, while that gives my content some authority, it doesn't make me a speaker.

I used to be a dreadful speaker — and I mean *dreadful*. Fortunately, I had the opportunity to practice in front of small groups, at meetings and workshops — and I took every opportunity I got to practice. I did Toastmasters for a while — it's a really good forum for developing your speaking skills from the beginner level up. It's a truly great place to start.

As I began to take the speaking path seriously I went out and did some intensive training for improvised theatre. I wanted to be able to continue speaking confidently when the sound system failed, when the lights went out, or when the next speaker was a last minute no-show. I wanted to be conscious of what it takes to engage an audience and keep them focussed till I leave the stage, and I wanted to have my performance skills honed into my sub-conscious so I could concentrate on my content.

The improv training built my strengths and covered my weaknesses. I've never been good at sticking to the script — but I knew I needed to be damn good with the skills if I was going to free-range and follow the audience interest, embellish the themes developed in a conference, and contribute my part to the 'light and shade' of an event.

I'm extremely passionate about my content — and take it very seriously — but I'm also aware that I'm there to support the show.

How do you customise your presentation to meet the needs of the audience?

I like to do as much research as possible before a gig. I will speak to as many people in the organising committee, management and events team as I can to understand what they want out of the event — and to understand the attendees and what they are likely to respond to.

I do independent research to get a broader and personalised view of what strategic shifts are going on for the attendees, for their organisations and for their markets/networks. The more I can understand their issues, how they see them, and how my content will apply to them, the better the performance will be.

And, finally, I'll often check in with the audience during the presentation. A little bit of question and answer, a show of hands, or a bit of audience response helps break up a crowded conference program — and can give me what I need to know to align with the audience in front of me.

What exercises do you do to relax before a presentation?

I do a variety of vocal and physical warm-ups that I've learned through theatre training. I think it's important to put on a great performance. Great content alone isn't enough — people respond to the physical, emotional and auditory presence as much as the subject matter.

So what do you talk about?

I talk about how organisations, communities and marketplaces function. I use living systems thinking to give insight into the behaviour we see every day inside our organisations. I teach people how as individuals they can make meaningful change happen in these organisations, in these living systems.

I show people how to exert personal leadership from where they are, without control, authority or power, by positively influencing in a living systems paradigm. If they're waiting for someone else to let them do something they're not leading, they're finding excuses. All anyone can ever change is his or her own behaviour, and all change that has ever happened has been achieved as a consequence of that. I teach people to exert meaningful influence in living organisations by changing their own behaviour.

I teach that no one owes his or her ideas a living. They need to make their ideas and their influence sustainable inside their organisation, to allow the organisation time to change around their ideas. I communicate how to exert influence beyond their own size: how to get organisations, networks and communities to change themselves.

I talk about the rules and structures that define an organisation — its governance — and how people can contribute to enhance governance to make themselves and their organisations have a greater capacity for achieving meaningful innovation on an ongoing basis.

As a speaker, what is the most common question you get asked and what is your answer to it?

I regularly get asked: "What is the one thing you would recommend people do to become successful." I'll admit here, just between you and me, that this question really annoys me! If there were only one thing that you needed to do, then everyone would do it. I'm always tempted to say, "You need to stop dumbing things down and stop looking for simple answers" — but I don't think that's a constructive response. Most of the time, I resist the temptation.

My usual response — hopefully a more constructive approach — is to come back to personal motivation and encourage people to reframe how they see themselves. I point out that the only thing you can change is your own behaviour, and that every change that ever happened, happened as a result of someone changing their own behaviour.

I'll quote Albert Einstein: "Insanity is doing the same thing and expecting a different outcome," and suggest people start with how they present themselves to the world. I recommend they take the understanding they've developed from my insights into living systems thinking and work out what role they want to play in that. I suggest they think about how they "inhabit" the role they are currently in, and how they could re-present themselves to be more effective in that role.

The one thing people should do is the only thing that anyone can do — change, grow, enhance and empower yourself!

The one thing people should do is the only thing that anyone can do — change, grow, enhance and empower yourself!

What have you found are the best methods or strategies for keeping motivated and focussed?

I'm really focussed on the difference I can make to my clients, the people in my audience and the organisations they work for. I'm driven to help people and organisations achieve their potential.

There's so much potential out there — in individual untapped skills and passions, and in organisations' hidden strengths and market opportunities. The faster the economy moves the more opportunity there is.

I love working with people who are prepared to grow. I love igniting that willingness to grow and to see opportunity — to help them reach out and overcome the perceptions they have of their own frustrations and limitations.

Do you continue to practice your personal development even now?

You always need to keep learning if you want to stay fresh. The opportunity to keep learning and expose myself to new challenges is one of the main reasons I love this career!

Most recently I took a refresher course with a guy called Toby Travanner. He runs a course for those wanting to get onto the professional speaker circuit, or current speakers wanting to refresh their skills. It's always good to hone your skills and I would recommend Toby to anyone who is serious about their speaking career.

What do you think stops people from achieving the level of success they desire?

In my experience, everyone comes pre-programmed with some form of self-limiting thinking. People who don't try things are limited by a fear of failure. People try everything only to find themselves limited by a fear of success!

It takes time, a thirst for life experience, a love of learning and constant work to expand and extend yourself, break out of your own shell, build a new one and repeat.

How fast or how far you move in any one step, and how long you wait between steps is entirely up to you.

Everyone comes pre-programmed with some form of self-limiting thinking. People who don't try things are limited by a fear of failure.

What business are you in and what services does it offer?

I brand myself as "The Innovation Coach." I help people, teams and organisations improve their capacity for innovation — for successfully investing in their own future.

Elite sportsmen have coaches who help them hone their skills, enhance their strengths and address their weaknesses — and yet, when it comes to business we're very shy to talk about achieving peak performance. Innovation coaching is for everyone who needs to lift innovation performance for their team, their organisation, their leadership practices and themselves.

Coaching fits targeted skills growth to specific needs. Like a sports coach, I identify the next step in an organisation's developmental journey — based on the needs, challenges, strengths and weaknesses identified in a holistic context.

Like the "sports science" revolution before it, I take a measured holistic view of the environment: the future, the competition, the organisational capacity for innovation, the people, the practices, the technology opportunities, the governance and more — to help get the very best out of investments, initiatives, teams, organisations and individuals.

The world is moving too fast to be operating below peak performance. I provide organisations with better ways to get ahead than just trying to learn through the trial and error of experience — using elite business coaching for elite business outcomes.

Everyone comes pre-programmed with some form of self-limiting thinking. People who don't try things are limited by a fear of failure.

What is your approach to marketing and how did you get your name out into the marketplace?

Reference selling is the strongest way to sell. In the early days I would find any excuse to get in front of an audience and then use social media channels to make sure people knew about it.

Event managers want a safe pair of hands. Reliability — not screwing up and making them look bad — is even more important than your content. Nothing speaks success like a track record and testimonials. You can't shortcut it. But you should amplify it. Find a stage. Promote your success.

Do you buy lottery tickets? Why or why not?

No. Just look at the numbers.

Fiona Craig

Fiona Craig

**99% Back Down When
The Going Gets Tough**

Fiona was born in Scotland in 1972 and lived there until 1999 when she fulfilled her dream of moving to Sydney, Australia.

She started her career in the legal profession, practicing corporate law with a prestigious Glaswegian firm, before transferring to another well-known firm in Sydney.

Her passion for people (and dislike of legislation and document drafting) saw her leave law in 1999 to pursue a very successful 10-year career in recruitment.

Upon selling the business in 2006, Fiona "found" her passion for coaching, mentoring and speaking while spending 12 months in the Byron Bay hinterland.

She now runs a successful business in which she works with professional women helping them move up, on and forward in their careers, and with organisations helping them attract and retain high performing women.

Fiona loves presenting to and motivating professional women to step outside of their own limits and expectations, and those of society, and focus on creating a career and a life that they truly love.

Fiona has an LLB (Hons), a Diploma in Coaching and is a Master Practitioner in NLP. She lives in Brisbane with her partner, Jason and their son, Struan.

How did you build your confidence as a speaker?

Growing up in Scotland, where I went to primary school, the Principal had a real passion for musical theatre.

Each year he directed the most amazing Gilbert & Sullivan musicals (by primary school standards anyway!) and I played parts from around age 8 or 9.

By the time I was ready for high school, I was playing lead parts — singing on stage in front of around 200 people — and. in a production of The Pirates of Penzance, I even had to peck a teacher on the cheek (the humiliation!).

I used to get teased mercilessly by my four older brothers and kids at school — in fact, I was probably bullied in today's terminology — but I loved it. I was never a brilliant singer but something happened to me when I was on stage. I went into 'flow' — as author Sir Ken Robinson calls it, I was truly in my Element.

I believe this is where I built my inner confidence to be on stage and in front of people.

What's your advice for a new and emerging speaker to find 'guest' speaker spots?

So many networking groups, associations and business groups are looking for guest speakers. I suggest starting with the associations in your field of expertise — for me it's legal associations such as The Law Society and any women's groups such as Women in Finance.

I use the association's website to find a relevant contact, then I connect with them on LinkedIn. They can then see my profile and my updates so that they get to know a little about my background. I'll then send an inmail introducing myself and offering to buy the contact a coffee to talk about their events and how I can contribute. It's a good 'opener.'

Also, make sure you are linked up to any sites that provide details of speaking or PR events such as www.sourcebottle.com.au in Australia.

Did you always know the career path you wanted to take? If not, where did you start from and how did you make the change?

At high school I loved English and all the Arts subjects. I decided early on I wanted to be a journalist. I was talked out of that by a teacher who told me I was 'too bright' to be a journalist and should think about studying law.

After 5 years of studying I got a job in a prestigious corporate law firm. I knew the second I sat at my desk on my very first day that it wasn't right for me.

Eventually, after moving to Australia, I also moved out of law into professional recruitment. The fast paced, people-focussed nature of the role really suited me and I had a ball for many years. However, the lack of variety bored me, and I felt very stagnant in terms of my personal development, which is when I decided to study coaching.

I started my own business after finishing my coaching qualification and, though it's been tough, I love it. I have the variety I want, working with incredible women and organisations that constantly challenge me to step up and be better today than I was yesterday.

What business are you in and what services does it offer?

I'm in the business of helping people create a career and life they love, and helping organisations develop a workplace culture where employees thrive and are fully engaged in their work.

My services are based around keynote speaking, training, mentoring and coaching in topics related to human behavior, and how we use it to improve our performance in work and in life.

Do you recall making a conscious decision to be a speaker? If so, when was it and why?

I knew I loved speaking in public right back in my school days. I was School Captain in high school and had to do lots of public speaking then — I always thrived on it and got great feedback.

During my Law degree I did a lot of legal debating. Although I got nervous, again I thrived on it.

I did an impromptu "best man" speech at my brother's wedding (because my other brother who was the best man was too nervous to speak!) And I insisted on breaking with tradition and doing a speech at my own wedding.

So I guess it was in the blood!

Then for the first 14 years of my career — in law and recruitment — I didn't really have the opportunity to do much speaking. But whenever I was given the chance, I jumped at it. The real breakthrough came for me a couple of years into running my own business. I was giving a keynote to a group of 100 lawyers. TOUGH audience.

The hour flew past — they loved me — and I came off the stage elated. Right then I vowed I would do as much speaking in my business as I possibly could.

Who was your first mentor or inspiration? Was it in person or through books/CDs/seminars?

I think my first mentor was my primary school Principal. He taught me that while I may not have amazing raw talent, confidence on stage would make up for what I lacked in that department.

I credit him with allowing me the platform to explore what is actually my number one strength — communication — at a very early stage in my life. I've never forgotten that experience and am thankful to this day that he guided me, even pushed me a little, into those roles.

What does success mean to you and how does one achieve it?

Success — ah, what a word!

My version and definition of success has changed dramatically over the years. I come from a very down-to-earth, hard-working Scottish family, who were extremely proud of me when I became the first in the family to graduate from university. That was success back then.

It used to be about money, too. Now, success to me is feeling I have the freedom to run a business doing work I love, with people I love, in ways that I love (to quote one of my mentors, Matt Church), and balance that with my family life.

What do you believe are the essential qualities or personal attributes of a successful person?

Humility, empathy, drive, energy and resilience are some of the key factors of success. Many of the women I work with astound me every day. They achieve so much by acting in alignment with their personal values and integrity.

What do you think stops people from achieving the level of success they desire?

I think there are a few key things that stop people. The first is fear. Fear of not being good enough, fear of being successful, fear of not getting it right... so many fears that get in the way of us fulfilling our true potential.

The second is expectation. Many of us expect too much or too little of ourselves. This gets in the way of us living a truly successful life.

Then there are the social expectations. We're brought up to fit in, do as we are told and, in most cases, get a 'good job' that pays well and keeps us secure.

We're taught to play safe and not take risks. Yet, you find the most successful people in life have taken many risks along the way.

One quote sums up how I feel about what stops people achieving the level of success they desire: "The enemy of a great life is a good life."

The enemy of a great life is a good life.

What can people do to stay on track, especially when times get tough?

Keep showing up! One of my mentors when I was training in coaching used to say this all the time. She said that 99% of the population would back down and not show up when the going got tough. The 1% who keeps showing up, doing the work, trying new things, failing fast and implementing what they learn, reaps the rewards.

99% of the population backs down and won't show up when the going gets tough. The 1% who keeps showing up, doing the work, trying new things, failing fast and implementing what they learn, reaps the rewards.

What are your five tips for reaching greater levels of success?

1. **Understand yourself** — inside out, back to front, upside down. You must know what motivates you, drives you, brings you down and buoys you up.

2. **Know and use your strengths.** Work with a coach and use strength profiling to be come crystal clear on what your natural talents are and how to use them even more every day to become a better version of yourself

3. **Never forget where you come from.** Your family and upbringing have given you your values, beliefs and outlook on life. Acknowledge that — change the beliefs that hold you back — but always remember where you started in life. It has given you more than you will ever realise.

4. **Take other people with you.** It can be lonely at the top.

5. **Just keep showing up.**

What is the most you have ever spent on a single purchase? For example: a pair of fabulous shoes or a totally indulgent toy (car/bike/boat etc.). Can you tell us about this item and why you bought it?

I bought a pair of boots on a trip back to Glasgow a few years ago. They were in a store called Pied a Terre and they cost GBP350, which in Australian dollars at that time was around $700.

I completely fell in love with the slightly vintage style and color — gorgeous orange-tan — I wore them to death for five years until they no longer fitted me after pregnancy. I was gutted, as they just got better with age!

Do you buy lottery tickets? Why or why not?

I don't buy lottery tickets because I don't believe in luck. I believe we create our own success in life — statistics and probability make up the rest.

If you could go back in time and meet your 16-year-old self, what would you tell her?

I'd tell her to back herself, completely and fully — every time. I'd tell her that her gut feeling is usually right, and that she should follow it, as often as she can.

I'd also let her know she doesn't have to do what others expect of her — that she is smart and talented enough to follow her own path and make a success of it. I'd suggest she travel more, dream bigger and set goals that stretch her — because she's capable of achieving them.

And finally, I'd say that no matter how much she protests she will never have children, having her son will be the biggest life-changing event she can ever imagine, and she will experience love like she has never known the second he is born.

Julie-Anne Black

Julie-Anne Black

**Be Genuine With Your Audience
and Win Every Time**

Julie-Anne (Julie-Anne) first appeared on TV when she was eight. At 19, she managed a modeling agency before landing a role as a TV production assistant at 23. Soon after her 24th birthday, she was appointed the role of producer for The Price Is Right and quickly became known as the 'Queen of Quiz.'

She produced an array of light entertainment hits, including Who Wants To Be A Millionaire, and was a production manager for the Sydney Olympics Opening Ceremony. Julie-Anne has worked with some of Australia's favourite stars, including Ray Martin, Eddie McGuire, Marcia Hines, Julia Morris and Larry Emdur.

When she was producing TV, she thought she was living the dream, but internally she was on a personal rollercoaster where she didn't feel she had a voice of influence and kept doubting and second-guessing herself. She hungered to be a charismatic communicator, self-assured and confident.

Since 2000, Julie-Anne has been dedicated to unearthing how and why we think the way we do and she's recognised communication is a system — it's a skill to be mastered.

As the founder of Be Brilliant Now, her research has taken her all around the world leading dynamic training programs that inspire thousands to be bold and irresistible communicators in life and business. Her signature programs, books and products combine her expertise as a mind-set, body language and NLP trainer with the secrets she learned as a top TV producer.

She has spoken on stages in New York, Los Angeles and Las Vegas and been featured in publications including CLEO, MX and Executive PA.

Do you suffer from nerves and if so how do you manage them?

Moving from behind the scenes as a TV producer to being in front of the audience was a daunting experience at first. I used to get so nervous and scared to present that I would pray for people not to enrol and turn up. It seems so silly now, but seven years ago, it was very real!

There was an endless list of things I was nervous about: I wouldn't do a good job, I'd forget my words, stumble over myself and be embarrassed. I was scared my audience wouldn't receive any value because I couldn't articulate my message, which of course meant I'd be laughed at and consequently feel like a fraud.

The pit of my stomach would churn, my mouth would dry up and my hands would shake from all the adrenalin pumping through my body because fight and flight mode had kicked into high gear. All the knowledge I depended on would disappear from my mind while my inner dialogue couldn't shut up. It ran rampant telling me how bad it was going to be!

But in spite of my prayers, people kept enrolling, so I had to step up, face my fear head on and do it anyway. It was a steep learning curve and I learnt very quickly that preparation was king and repetition was queen.

To help me prepare for each presentation, I developed the following 3-step formula. It works because it helps me get out of my head and into my heart. It turns nervousness into excited anticipation, which is what provides fuel for your performance. And the process starts well before you even enter the venue to speak. The formula combines the secrets I used to get great performances from TV hosts with hot tips to future pace your desired outcome.

My mind still goes blank just before I hit the stage. But instead of dreading it, I know it's my unconscious way of clearing any unwanted clutter so I can be 100% available for my audience. After all, I've done the preparation and now they deserve my complete focus and attention. So just before I go on I remind myself, "this is about my audience, not me. Go out there and be passionate for them, share what you know so they can be brilliant now!"

Step 1: LIGHTS

When I was working with TV presenters, the first thing we did was plan and prepare their story by reverse engineering it. We'd start with the end in mind. Decide the outcomes you want your audience to receive and the value you wish to share. Plan your key points and tell stories to bring your message to life. Script your introduction and conclusion so you always know where to start and how to end.

Step 2: CAMERA

Looking through the lens of the camera, how is your audience responding to your message? The key here is to decide how you want your audience to feel at the conclusion of your presentation. For example, if you want your audience to leave feeling inspired then your message needs to be inspiring. Tweak your message until it represents the same emotional response you want to influence in your audience.

Step 3: ACTION

OK, you've crafted a message you love and you know the outcome for your audience; now it's time to step into the spotlight and be The Star.

To do that you need to ask yourself: "Who do I need to become to produce the desired outcome?" Then embody the character traits you'll need to give a powerful and convincing performance. Focus on being genuine with your audience and you'll win every time.

Remember if you want your audience to leave feeling inspired, your message needs to be inspiring and so do you! This means your signature style, body language, mannerisms, tone of voice, and smile all need to be transmitting the same intention.

 Focus on being genuine with your audience and you'll win every time.

Once you've completed these steps, keep rehearsing and visualising yourself achieving the successful completion of the outcome you want. Play the scene out in your mind exactly as you intend it to be. Then the moment before you take center stage, be encouraging, remind yourself it's about your audience not you and they deserve your best. You can handle it, then go on and be brilliant now.

What do you believe are the top 5 attributes of a successful speaker?

The successful presenters and TV stars I've worked with over the years all have similar attributes in common, which when distilled, are what set them apart and make them great. In fact, I have a saying:

> "Being a Bold and Irresistible Communicator is a lot like producing a hit TV show. You'll be a ratings success or flop depending on how you connect and engage with your audience."

As Maya Angelou said:

> "I've learned that people will forget what you said, people will forget what you did, but people will never forget how you made them feel."

And the most successful speakers always leave their audiences feeling like they can achieve it, too.

The top 5 attributes, I believe a successful speaker possesses include:

1. Your ability to TELL STORIES that captivate, educate and inspire

1. Your CONNECTION with your message

2. Your ENGAGEMENT with your audience

3. Your PASSION about your topic of expertise

4. Your desire to be IRRESISTIBLY YOU.

 "... People will forget what you said, people will forget what you did, but people will never forget how you made them feel." — Maya Angelou

Did you always know the career path you wanted to take? If not, where did you start from and how did you make the change?

When I was a child, I loved goofing around in front of the camera and it was awesome to have the opportunity to do some modeling in those early years. During my school holidays, I would opt to work as a casting director assistant so my transition to become a TV Producer felt like a natural progression.

But there was always something niggling inside of me, something left untapped, unresolved, unanswered. The truth was, I always wanted to be in front of the camera but never had the confidence. So it felt safer to stay behind the scenes.

It wasn't until I stepped on stage to do a presentation on the 'power of words' that I really unearthed how much I loved it — the buzz was terrifying and exhilarating at the same time. Drawing on my TV experience, I dissected what the great TV presenters did and studied hundreds of people to see what made them such great communicators.

For me, making the transition meant I had to start believing I could. So I spent countless hours practicing in front of the mirror, with friends, my dog, teaching classes, putting myself in situations outside my comfort zone. I'd volunteer to be the demonstration model if a speaker needed it — any opportunity to be on stage.

Basically, it takes consistency, hard work, an unforeseeable amount of hours behind the scenes, and a hell-of-a-lot of encouragement along the way. With repetition being the mother of all skills, keep persevering until it becomes a natural part of what you do.

What business are you in and what services does it offer?

I'm the founder of a training company called Be Brilliant Now. We specialise in showing emerging leaders and entrepreneurs how to be 'Bold and Irresistible Communicators' by getting them 'performance ready' for the boardroom, media appearances and speaking gigs.

We show you how to step into the spotlight with a message that inspires and body language that influences so you feel charismatic, confident and at ease in front of any audience.

Our clients typically come to us for three key reasons:

1. They struggle to express themselves as an expert in their field

2. Their uncertainty sabotages their confidence to connect and engage

3. They're working hard only to realise they're missing out on cool opportunities

Our mission is to deliver powerful tools to boost confidence and unleash superstar appeal so you can become the star performer in life and business you know you were born to be.

What have been your highlights in speaking?

There have been so many brilliant times in my speaking career so far. Highlighting my top 3 wow moments would have to include:

1. Having audience members moved to tears because something I said inspired them to change their thinking on the spot. There's something so awe-inspiring when people come up to me and share their story, telling me that my courage to share mine turned a light for them — "if she can do it, so can I."

2. There was one man in particular who went home after my presentation and said to his wife he may have found someone who could help his or her troubled son. Michael and I worked together for around 12 months. When he arrived he was suicidal, at the lowest point in his life. By the end he had graduated as a horticulturalist with high distinctions, his brother and he had become friends and he genuinely loved his life — he was happy. We never truly know the impact we can have on others, which is why its so important to live our life purpose with as much love, passion and dedication as we can.

3. I was the closing speaker at a seminar in Los Angeles, my first presentation in the US. I'd heard they loved Aussies but could never have imagined the response.

4. We'd been in the conference for two days and I felt we needed to crank things up a notch! So I opened my talk playing the song, 'Let's Get It Started' by the Black Eyed Peas. I got everyone on their feet dancing, instantly creating a party atmosphere.

5. Settling into my presentation, I remember looking out on the audience and feeling such a state of bliss to be there in that moment. There was so much audience participation, laughter, aha moments — it felt incredible that I could influence such a powerful response in people. I was overwhelmed with tears of joy as I received my

first standing ovation. I remember thinking to myself: this is what it's like when you get to truly connect with your tribe. AMAZING!

6. I feel so blessed everyday to be travelling the world sharing the stage with other inspiring speakers.

What are your secrets to being a top speaker and presenter?

There are some practical steps that I put in place to ensure I share high value, feel confident and have fun. After lots of trial and error I've created a little ritual that helps me consistently deliver:

1. **Make connections** and develop relationships with key people who need what you do.

2. **Know your audience intimately** — what are they trying to get done?

3. **Craft the message** you know your audience will love to hear as well as loving the content you want to share

4. **Have fun** getting creative with how to present your message in the most powerful and impactful way

5. **Take time to design and craft stories**, exercises and anecdotes that illustrate your message in an engaging, innovative and inspiring way to produce great value for your audience.

6. **Did I say have fun!** It's worth saying again — having fun and being passionate about your topic of expertise. One of my key points is to demonstrate techniques that are practical, easy to master and can produce instant results giving them a little win right now.

7. **Be yourself** — give yourself permission to share your personality and cheekiness, giving the best of you to your audience.

Do you continue to practice your personal development even now?

Personal development is super important for me because it keeps me fresh. It inspires me and helps me stay centered and work through any of my own inner gunk that presents itself. I love to learn — and with so many talented people with amazing things to share, I'm always on the hunt for new and creative ways of thinking and communicating.

Plus, I believe walking your talk is essential to being authentic. You'll often see me in the audience, participating in programs or with an empowering audio book playing on my headset as I set out for an early morning or sunset run.

My philosophy is — if I'm teaching you how to present like a superstar, I'd better be on stage doing it myself as well as researching the best of the best so I can fast track the brilliance directly to you.

Is there a significant quote or saying that you live by?

- I love quotes and have so many that I draw upon in different moments. Here a few of my favorites: "Nothing is impossible; the word Itself says "I'm possible!" — Audrey Hepburn

- "Respond to every call that excites your spirit." — Rumi

- "Be a first rate version of yourself, not a second rate version of someone else." — Judy Garland

- "All our dreams can come true — if we have the courage to pursue them." — Walt Disney

- "Let me tell you something you already know. The world ain't all sunshine and rainbows. It's a very mean and nasty place and I don't care how tough you are it will beat you to your knees and keep you there permanently if you let it. You, me, or nobody is gonna hit as hard as life. But it ain't about how hard you're hit. It's about how hard you can get it and keep moving forward. How much you can take and keep moving forward. That's how winning is done! Now if you know what you're worth then go out and get what you're worth. But ya gotta be willing to take the hits, and not pointing fingers saying you ain't where you wanna be because of him, or her, or anybody! Cowards do that and that ain't you! You're better than that! I'm always gonna love you no matter what. No matter what happens. You're my son and you're my blood. You're the best thing in my life. But until you start believing in yourself, ya ain't gonna have a life. Don't forget to visit your mother." — Rocky Balboa [Sylvester Stallone] in *Rocky* (2006)

If you could give just one piece of advice about speaking that would make the biggest difference in one persons life, what would that be?

Being on stage isn't actually about you; it's about your message and how it can help your audience achieve their dreams.

The part that is about you is making sure you give a performance that captivates, educates and influences your audience to take action and get results. To do this well you need to love what you do and give yourself permission to be irresistibly you.

What does success mean to you and how does one achieve it?

To me, success equals loving life, having fun and making a difference.

To be successful as a speaker you need to seize every opportunity to be on stage sharing your message. Put your hand up for free gigs, paid gigs, any gigs that have you talking in front of your ideal audience. Even when you present to an audience that isn't your target market, you will learn valuable lessons in being able to connect, engage and build rapport.

Raise your online profile with video so people can see, hear and get a sense of who you are. Remember people want to know you, like you and trust you before they'll buy you. Your community love knowing why you do what you do so share it with them.

Publish a book that delivers value and sets you up as 'The Star' in your industry and then leverage your book with everything you've got.

Constantly connect with people asking for opportunities to speak and present. Target specific niches and look out for problem areas where your expertise can provide specific solutions. Your success depends on how your market responds to you.

 Put your hand up for free gigs, paid gigs, any gigs that have you talking in front of your ideal audience.

What do you think stops people from achieving the level of success they desire?

Mindset is the single most powerful trait that prevents people from achieving the level of success they desire. I see it all the time — people fighting for their limitations, arguing about why they shouldn't, couldn't, won't. Their internal dialogue goes nuts, constantly repeating stories to sabotage and doubt their own abilities.

In TV, there are scriptwriters to create particular scenes for us. In life, too. What's cool is you're the one with the pen. You get to edit your disempowering beliefs and rewrite your story so it's exactly as you want it to be.

What can people do to stay on track, especially when times get tough?

Remember your WHY!

I work on with my students and clients to unpack their mission:

- Why are you particularly well suited to doing what you do?
- Why is it so important for you to step into the spotlight and share a message that helps people solve their problems?
- Why do you want to inspire and influence?

When you've nailed this, even in the darkest days your mission will always shine light. As Mahatma Gandhi said: "A small body of determined spirits fired by an unquenchable faith in their mission can alter the course of history."

What are your tips for reaching greater levels of success?

My eight principles for producing greater levels of success are:

1. Know your outcome.

2. Believe in your vision with your whole heart. Be passionate.

3. Take inspired action every day towards your outcome.

4. Have sensory acuity. Be aware — look, hear, feel and know what results you are getting.

5. Have behavioral flexibility. If you're not getting the results you want, adjust your plan and 'course correct' accordingly.

6. Operate from a physiology and psychology of excellence.

7. Celebrate, Reward, Reflect and Review.

8. Re-focus and commence the process again.

What keeps you from retiring and lying on the beach every day?

I love what I do. Plus I'm on a mission to inspire millions to be bold and irresistible communicators in life and business. I believe there's never been a better time to feel inspired and wowed about your own capacity to be brilliant now.

Jesper Jurcenoks

Don't be a speaker to "be someone"
Be a speaker to "do something"

Jesper "JJ" Jurcenoks was born in Odense, Denmark in 1968. He got his first regular job at age 11 working in a toy-store — a job he kept for 4 years. At 12, he was also running the fruit and snack bar at his school, earning a profit for that year's field trip.

By 13, he was buying Rubik's cubes directly from the distributor and selling them for profit, while impressing people demonstrating the solution.

At 14 Jesper entered evening school in computer programming and his world has never been the same since. He sold his first computer game at 15, and by then the toy store had been replaced by a computer store.

At 18 Jesper returned from Switzerland having completed his 3-year secondary education in only two years, to finish his academic degree 1 year later as both the youngest in his class and top of class.

Fast Forward to 1995. After six years in increasingly advanced computer jobs in both international Shipping and HP, Jesper started his first groups of companies in Copenhagen with a systems integrator and ISP, which he sold in 2001. Since leaving school, "JJ" had pioneered the use of innovative technologies from satellite email over thin client to WiMax, in both Europe and North America.

In 2002, Jesper set his sights on the American Dream and the new field of computer vulnerability Assessment, relocating his family to the US in 2003, and founding netVigilance Inc. that same fall.

After 10 very rewarding years in netVigilance, JJ has relinquished daily operation of netVigilance to jump into the emerging field of security intelligence, joining his good friends at Critical Watch as Director for Security Research and Chief Evangelist. Taking an engineering approach to PR, sales and marketing, Jesper has come full circle from sales as a kid over 30 years in computer engineering and now back to sales and marketing.

Jesper lives in Oakland, California with his wife and youngest daughter. He is the chairman of the non-profit crime-prevention organisation, Neighborhood Guard.

What business are you in and what services does it offer?

I educate decision makers on the emerging area of "Security Intelligence" — the branch of computer security that creates order in the face of information overload and then automatically applies that to better use of existing data security tools like firewall and anti-virus software.

What do you believe are the top 5 attributes of a successful speaker?

1. **Humility**. Even the most knowledgeable person in the world on a subject is still learning, still seeking the truth

2. **Confidence**. Try not to shake as you present

3. **Engagement**. Keep eye-contact with your audience, and don't speak in monotone! Change the pitch and volume of your speaking voice

4. **Liveliness**. I don't like to hide behind a podium. I love my wireless slide clicker and laser pointer. I always remove the microphone from its stand and move around the stage

5. **Smiling and laughter.** It's an undervalued attribute of a great speaker. Laugh at yourself — but don't make fun of the audience.

How did you build you confidence as a speaker?

No matter if I'm talking to 40 people or 200, I always pick four to five audience members and speak to them specifically.

Once I get started, I always notice a few people who are more receptive to me that others. These people smile back to me, follow me with their eyes all the time, and they laugh at my jokes. Ignore the guy in the corner who looks like he has fallen asleep, and the girl checking her email. Speak directly to the most rapt audience members.

Once I'm mentally speaking to only four to five people the whole mood in the room becomes more intimate. The fear of looking like an idiot in front of 200 people is gone and I feed off the positive feedback I get from these select people. I look to them for cues to whether I need to go into more detail or if I should move forward. Without these reference points I feel like I'm drifting in the ocean.

I recently gave my first webinar presentation. I had 35 people online listening to me, but they were all muted and I couldn't see them. I was alone on the line, talking into dead silence. Without feedback I totally lost my bearings. It was a terrible experience. Next time I plan to clearly visualise a few key audience members so I can mentally direct my presentation.

How do you customise your presentation to meet the needs of the audience?

When adapting an existing presentation, my minimum preparation is updating the date and title slide to reflect the name of the new audience. People like to feel you're talking specifically for them.

If I know anything about my audience I'll review the presentation against their specific concerns and goals. In the autumn of 2012 and spring of 2013, I gave my crime prevention presentation 36 times. Sometimes I was asked to deliver a 15-minute overview, other times I was required to give a detailed 2.5-hour presentation. I pick and choose from 50+ slides to cover the specific concerns of each neighborhood.

Do you have a product, program or other offering that you present for sale at speaking events? Do you recommend this for new speakers?

You presented to 40 people last night. So what do you have to show for it? How many bought from you? How many email addresses did you get? Who cares if you handed out 30 CDs with your MP3s — how will you follow up on the potential customer without their email addresses?

What's your advice for a new and emerging speaker to find 'guest' speaker spots?

If you want to find guest-speaking spots, hit the local meeting groups, or check out meetup.com. PS: It is surprisingly easy to get on the radio.

If you want to find guest-speaking spots, hit the local meeting groups, or check out meetup.com.

What do you believe it takes to be a professional speaker?

Don't be a speaker to "be someone." Be a speaker to "do something."

Set a goal of how you want to help people and decide how you'll measure when you reach that goal. Only then determine if speaking will help you. The speaking part should be a means to an end, never the end in itself. While it helps the nerves if you like being the center of attention, that should not be your reason for speaking. Your audience will see you as self-promoting, arrogant or vain.

What have been your highlights in speaking?

It was a good day when I was covered on the front page of the San Francisco Chronicle with the words "no one received more applause than Jesper "JJ" Jurcenoks."

Do you continue to practice your personal development even now?

I *want* to practice personal development every day, but in reality my prioritisation is still not strong enough to make that happen consistently. I know that, if I 'm not improving, I'll soon be outdated in our constantly improving world.

Is there a significant quote or saying that you live by?

"If you want to build a ship, don't drum up people to collect wood and don't assign them tasks and work, but rather teach them to long for the endless immensity of the sea." — Antoine de Saint-Exupery

Did you ever want to 'give up' because it all got a bit too much?

Tasks ahead can often feel overwhelming. This is a sign of bad prioritising — if you feel this way it's time to:

1. Make a list of all the things to be done

2. Accept many of them won't be done

3. Know that this is OK.

What do you believe are the essential qualities or personal attributes of a successful person?

Humility, constructive paranoia, simplicity and discipline are the keys to success — it's that simple.

What do you think stops people from achieving the level of success they desire?

This really is true: you are your own worst enemy.

What stopped me from achieving my goals for a long time was a lack of clear goals! I know it feels like work, but you need a long-term smart goal. Where do you want to be in 15 years? How do you know if you have reached your goal? What milestones do you have to reach on the way to get there? Are these milestones realistic?

What can people do to stay on track, especially when times get tough?

It's very easy to let your guard down and slip back into the comfort zone. When this happens, revisit your visualisation exercises to get your focus back on your priorities.

What are your five tips for reaching greater levels of success?

Five tips for greater success:

1. Read David Allen's *Getting Things Done*

2. Read Jim Collins' (in this order) *Good to Great, Built to Last, How the Mighty Fall,* and *Great By Choice.*

3. Attend Tony Robbins' "Unleash the Power Within."

4. Lose those pounds NOW. Over the years, I gained a lot of weight and became pre-diabetic. Once I had fully visualised my goal of a thin, healthy version of myself, I lost 60 pounds in 4 months, 100% reversed my pre-diabetes and got my BMI down to 20. My wife thinks my new 'thin' me, is super-hot. Honestly how can anybody look to you for advice if you can't even manage your own body? How can you trust yourself to achieve your goals if you can't even figure out how to achieve your body goal?

5. Make sure to set those SMART goals.

The most important advice I've received was from my chairman in net-Vigilance. He said to me: "There will always be more tasks than time. The day you accept you won't be able to do everything you want to do is the day you can really start to move forward."

What keeps you from retiring and lying on the beach every day?

I lived on a tropical island in the Bahamas in 2007-2008. It's not all it's made up to be. I like California much better.

Karen Ostenried

Karen Ostenried

Feedback is the breakfast of champions

Karen was born in Darwin in 1962 and started her career as singer at 15. She has been a professional entertainer in Australia and overseas for 30 years, while quietly becoming accomplished in medical research.

She has worked in Australia's most prestigious medical research institutes and was invited to work at Heidelberg's German Cancer Research Centre at 23. Afterwards she became one of a handful of Australians skilled in Transgenic and Knockout technologies. She was the first person to produce a transgenic NOD model in the early 1990s and was persuaded to move to Perth in 2000 to help establish a highly specialised biomedical company, which became a multimillion-dollar business in four years.

Karen has spoken to scientists and the general public as an educator and motivator and has trained all levels, from cleaners to directors.

Realising there are many brilliant people working hard to achieve success in their passion but struggling to convey their message to the world, she now trains entrepreneurs to shine. This is a great way of branding and leveraging their time for maximum exposure to the world.

Karen takes the skills she gleaned from communicating on stage to the business world in a unique way. It's not about acting, but being comfortable and confident in unusual environments.

Her knowledge of biology, combined with stage experience and fascination with psychology and behavior drives her to refine and fast track individuals to present authentically.

A member of the local Landcare group, former President of the Arts Alliance and several other community groups, Karen established "The Kinglake Phoenix Singers" following the 2009 Black Saturday bushfires to assist in the psychological recovery.

Soon to publish her book, "10 Steps for Stage Success," Karen still lives in Kinglake with her husband and horses.

Do you suffer from nerves and if so how do you manage them?

I don't know anyone who doesn't suffer from some sort of nerves before speaking however, it is possible to manage them and make them work for you rather than against you.

Only one time I didn't feel nervous — and this was when I realised I was in severe shock. I was doing a fundraiser for the Black Saturday fires, which killed hundreds of people and devastated multiple communities in Australia.

Now I manage nerves in a multipronged fashion by:

1. Having a disciplined preparation

2. Visualisation and affirmations

3. Breathing and relaxation techniques

4. Mindset, including self-talk management.

 Make nerves work for you rather than against you.

What do you believe are the top 5 attributes of a successful speaker?

1. Being engaging

2. Being funny

3. Being authentic

4. Being professionally prepared

5. Being a storyteller.

How did you build you confidence as a speaker?

I rehearse, record and improve until I'm completely happy with the words, voice, body language and energy. By this time I will be running on autopilot. I also try to video all my performances and review them, taking note of what got good responses. I ask for honest, no-holds-barred feedback from experts, explaining that I believe in continuous improvement and will not take it personally. As Clinton Swaine says, "Feedback is the breakfast of champions."

Do you have a product, program or other offering that you present for sale at speaking events? Do you recommend this for new speakers?

I do an audience event assessment so I find out as much as possible about the group, especially what their biggest problem is.

From there you can identify a process to remove this problem. If I'm doing an inspirational speech I will definitely create an opening to experience some of what I've experienced, so they can access the emotion for themselves. I also find out my audience demographic to make sure the material and references I use are familiar to them. Depending on the content I would hope to inspire with emotion or add humour, stories and examples.

 Confidence is like a magnet. People are drawn to it like moths to a flame.

Did you always know the career path you wanted to take? If not, where did you start from and how did you make the change?

I didn't always know I was going to be a speaker. I was good at debating at school and loved to be on the unpopular side just for the hell of it.

Throughout my science career I saw many great and terrible presentations. In fact, my long time boss and good friend, Professor Jacques F Miller, was a brilliant scientist, speaker, teacher and influencer, but he was unbelievably struck by anxiety prior to speaking. He really hated it but knew it was part of the business. I thought this so strange. At the time I was refining my stage performances every week in pubs and loved entertaining an audience.

Another well-known professor, Gustav Nossal, was amazing at translating complex science into simple-to-understand English and making it sound exciting. He made a point of remembering names, treating everyone as equal everywhere he went, and yet he was humble, strong and confident — great qualities in a speaker.

I realised the ability of a leader to effectively communicate and persuade team members to "buy-in" plays a huge roll in a team's success. You'll position yourself in a far more successful place if you use the correct language and jargon when dealing with different levels of hierarchy. Then I learned using clean humour or creativity made me even more successful in influencing others.

I had to give somewhat boring content training seminars to scientists so wanted to make it fun and interesting. When I was lecturing about how to move through a bio-secure facility I used the theme of Moses and the 10 Commandments of Bio-security ("Thou shalt not enter without first," "if doing X, ye shall enter the gates of hell and never be allowed near heaven again"). It worked. They remembered the content because they were "entertrained."

I suddenly understood that my life would be fulfilling if I could take what I'd learned about body language, and communication from my many years on stage, (communicating a story in song and have an audience totally enthralled) and empower people to present without fear by inspiring them to think or behave differently. The hidden bonus for what I was teaching was the gift of confidence. It's like a magnet — people are drawn to it like moths to a flame. Confidence in one area of your life also overflows into other areas.

Consider this. Two women go into a pub. One is confident in herself and her abilities, has a great career and is physically fit and healthy.

The other has a good career, is physically fit, pretty, but incomplete without a boyfriend.

Now imagine what their posture would look like. Who would be smiling and attracting all the attention? Even when she gets chatting with people and passes the conversation over to her insecure friend, the guys go back to the one who is standing upright, proud and comfortable.

But the insecure woman can change the situation completely simply by changing her behavior, posture, facial expressions and her ideas about herself. I'm a firm believer of "Fake it before you make it." Scientifically, it's all about retraining the brain and muscle memory.

 Be humble, strong and confident — the qualities of a great speaker.

What makes you stand out from your competitors?

Most speakers don't coach presentation skills. Only a few of us have other stage skills such as singing or dancing. I came to this industry as a body language and voice expert — I love being on stage and in front of a camera.

I now love speaking equally as much as singing and coaching. I use games, fun challenges and over 70% hands-on exercises in my tool kit. Consequently my programs are strictly limited to small groups. It's been proven that having fun while learning helps you retain much more content than just memory alone.

I know my background as both a professional singer and scientist makes me unique. I draw on the skills of the entertainer to engage and hold an audience and deal with stage fright. I'll often open with a song specific for the audience or topic, which is a great attention getter. I'm able to read people's body language and the energy of the room very quickly and make changes fast if necessary.

I was already knowledgeable about personal presentation and branding prior to speaking. Being a vocal coach with a medical background gives me a clear understanding of the biomechanics. The thespian in me pushes my creativity. From science, which is 90% failure, I've learned to handle challenges and foster a "never give up" attitude. Most of all it has given me a huge training ground for problem solving and people skills.

Who was your first mentor or inspiration? Was it in person or through books/CDs/seminars?

My idol is Amanda Gore. I met her at a Bushfire Recovery Women's Retreat and she was the defining person in my decision to become an influential speaker.

Amanda has made a successful international career in the corporate world by bringing joy into the workplace and the personal lives of her audiences. She improves the workplace environment, which in turn increases productivity, and does it in a very professional, entertaining and humorous way.

As far as other influential people, I've listened to many interviews and presentations given by Brian Tracy, Jim Rohn, Benjamin J Harvey, John De Martini, Pat Mesiti, Peter J Daniels, and many other thought leaders on personal and financial development. I am a Global Institute for Extraordinary Women partner (GIFEW), I read countless books and listen to CDs on personal development, business and prosperity.

Do you have a mentor today? If so, who is it and why?

Mentors are a brilliant resource, guiding you through the unknown and saving you from making countless mistakes. I have different mentors for different areas, including marketing mentors (Taki Moore and Kerwin Rae), a speaker and life coach (Clinton Swaine) and specific business mentors.

Do you continue to practice your personal development even now?

I practice personal development constantly. It's part of my mantra of continuous improvement. The world and universe is constantly changing. To survive in any environment we must be sensitive to these changes and able to adapt and take advantage of them without jeopardising anyone. I find it funny that, in my early 20s, I didn't understand the term "enlightenment." Now I'm getting a handle on the process.

Did you ever want to 'give up' because it all got a bit too much?

Sure, there have been many times when I wanted to give up. In fact, I had every excuse to justify giving up. After the Black Saturday fires I had no home, no studio, no income, I lived in a decimated environment, was isolated and my computer skills were basic. We were taken advantage of in a vulnerable position, I was suffering post-traumatic stress, we were under-insured and in the chaos and confusion many people were behaving irrationally.

Prior to the disaster I heard Brian Tracy say, "whenever you find your purpose and life goal, life itself will come along and test how serious you are about it. It will slam you down and when you get up it will kick you down again and again and again, to see if you are really serious."

A line by Pat Mesiti also helped me. He said that everyone has their down days, even the most successful people don't have perfect lives. He quotes from Winston Churchill: "If you are going through hell, don't stop."

 Winston Churchill: "If you are going through hell, don't stop."

A great book by Spencer Johnson, *Peaks and Valleys,* describes the roller coaster of life and how to deal and prepare for it. It's essential to have a great support network. The hardest and biggest lesson I ever learned was to mix with great people and gather a championship team by asking for help.

 Nonverbal communication is over 75% of all communication. That means what you do is more important than what you say.

What is the first step that someone could take if they decided to follow in your footsteps today?

- Go out and see as many speakers as possible. Don't just be inspired, analyze them and their speeches. How do they start; how do they connect with their audience? Research their habits

- Pick a coach, mentor or role model who is not only great on stage but off stage, too

- Invest in your future and don't wait to be perfect before you start

- Learn how to breathe diaphragmatically, stand tall and smile

- Be prepared to laugh at yourself.

What are your thoughts on body language?

Body language is so important to presentations because it tells the truth about your beliefs.

Nonverbal communication is over 75% of all communication. That means what you do is more important than what you say. The greatest tools you can use when becoming a speaker are a voice recorder more and video recorder. Your body tells the audience if you are serious and genuine about the words you are using. They can identify full commitment, desperation, celebration, or if you are hiding or holding something back.

Why is this important? People will only buy or invest in the person behind the business and the person they trust the most. If they see you holding back something through fear, you can be perceived as being untrustworthy. This is a very subtle language behind language, but it's the key to influence. Don't underestimate nonverbal cues. People who understand and can read nonverbal language hold great power.

People who understand and can read nonverbal language hold great power.

Was it hard to overcome your first major obstacle? What was it?

The hardest thing for me to overcome at the beginning was my self-worth.

I was moving into an industry unfamiliar to me. It was a challenge to sell my services on stage, close well from stage and promote myself. I had no copywriting experience and no cash flow to outsource anything. Phrases like, "I don't want to charge too much as I don't have much experience speaking" popped into my head. I lost a lot of confidence when the fires shattered my world.

I overcame all this by constantly feeding my success funnel (the material I was reading, listening to, people I hung around with, asking for help and being involved in business mastermind groups). I had to re-learn that it was OK to make mistakes and I applied all the things I teach my singing students to my life.

As a speaker, what is the most common question you get asked and what is your answer to it?

When I refer to the statement, "fake it until you make it," or "act like you are confident in order to get confidence," people often say that is being false and inauthentic.

My reply? Our body language often operates from the sympathetic nervous system (fight or flight mode) when fearful. It masks our true self. We all know this fear isn't helping us, so we need to retrain our sympathetic nervous system to exhibit a more relaxed and confident appearance. We're not changing who we are when we learn a new behavior. We're just accessing other characteristics and behaviors that we've not investigated before, but which maybe critical to revealing our authentic self to the world.

When we try something new it usually feels very uncomfortable and clumsy. Remember when you first learned to ride a bike? You were scared, wobbly and all over the place until you practiced enough. You might have even had a few crashes. But gradually you got better and before too long you were riding along singing a song and not even thinking about the biomechanics of your arms and legs.

Speaking and presenting is simply learning new skills that sometimes feel awkward at the beginning but will eventually become embedded in your body and mind. I never suggest people lie, falsify their facts or aspects of their presentations. You should never offer anything you can't deliver.

What can people do to stay on track, especially when times get tough?

When times are tough, being overwhelmed is a risk. Go back to the plan. If you don't have a plan, create one. Then work out who can help you achieve it.

Once your plan is crystal clear, make sure you've identified what recharges your soul. For me it's singing, or just spending time with nature and my horses. Set up your support network and call on them for help. Manage all aspects of your life including time, finances, fitness and health levels (stay as fit and well as you possibly can and never let this drop off, especially when times are tough), mindset and joy activities.

Cut out unnecessary things or people who deplete your energy and are basically negative. Keep a book of all your achievements to date and refer to it when you're down. And, if your dreams are worth fighting for… Never. Ever. Give Up. There's always a solution to every challenge.

Finally, remember there are people in this world with far greater challenges. Whenever possible give back to someone else. Be realistic and gentle on yourself. Baby steps.

 When times are tough, being overwhelmed is a risk. Go back to the plan. If you don't have a plan, create one.

Kate Burr

Humour is great for business

Kate Burr was born in Adelaide, South Australia in 1975 and is the "middle child" of three girls. After working a number of 'normal' jobs in banking, finance, government and education she finally listened to her 'inner voice' and tried her luck at stand up comedy.

In 2001 while living in the South Australian countryside, she entered her first comedy competition. She was so nervous she didn't tell anyone except her husband Jeff (just as she was about to get on the plane so he couldn't talk her out of it). Fortunately the performance was a success!

At her 2007 Fringe debut, when she finally decided to take herself 'seriously,' Kate was nominated as "Best Emerging Comedy" for her solo show "Back in 30 Minutes." She was also part of the cast for the sold-out show "Titters!" that won the Adelaide Fringe 'People's Choice Award.'

After a successful debut into the 'real world' of Comedy, Kate returned to her 'day job' as the Front Office Lady at a school, sat down at her desk and thought "this is soooo not right for me anymore!" Less than six months later she had quit her day job to pursue comedy full time.

Between becoming a mum, Kate has produced and performed comedy shows in six Adelaide Fringe festivals. Her talents have seen her perform in comedy clubs around Australia, international business conferences and host the inaugural GO festival in Melbourne, Australia. Kate also shares her knowledge with others, running Comedy workshops in association with Country Arts SA.

Kate is Australia's MUMber 1 Comedian. She is the creator of "Recharge Comedy Shows for Mums" and stars as the "Physically Stuffed Mum" in the multi-award nominated, comedy musical show "Three Stuffed Mums."

More than 7000 parents in over 90 performances have seen her hilarious 'mum-based' comedy. Kate's bubbly effervescent nature overflows on stage and she brings such a warm energy to the place it's hard not to feel better after seeing her perform.

Kate lives in Willunga with her husband Jeff and daughter Lily.

As a speaker, what is the most common question you get asked and what is your answer to it?

When people find out I'm a comedian I often get the response — "that must be the hardest job in the world! To do public speaking is hard, but to make them laugh as well, that's so brave! Do you get scared?"

I used to just laugh because I don't find it scary at all. You know how people jump out of planes and get all pumped at the end of it. Well that's like me after I do a performance — I love it, I get such an adrenaline rush.

But when I kept getting asked the question, it got me thinking. Why do people think it's so hard?

I think the answer is in most part that it's a process usually learned by trial and error (in front of a room full of drunk people — talk about a baptism of fire!) Most people aren't prepared (or stupid enough) to keep fronting up time after time until they get good.

And by the time you reach the status of "naturally funny" you aren't even conscious of what you are doing –it just comes instinctively. Often you aren't aware of all the steps you take, you just do it and it works. So it's really hard to find out how to do it unless you have a go.

It wasn't until I was commissioned by Country Arts SA to run a comedy workshop with two other comics that we had to break the process down and work out how to teach it. As it turns out, once you know what you're doing it's pretty easy.

I'll probably get in trouble with some of the other comedians in the industry because they think that comedy is an "art form" and you can't teach it. But we managed to teach a room full of women how to be funny and do stand up comedy. These women went from "I'm not funny, and I'm not even sure if I actually want to do this" to a standing ovation at the end of their show in only five weeks.

 Anyone can be funny. You just have to step up to the plate and claim the title!

What have you found to be the benefits of using humour in Presenting?

I love humour. It's said to be the great equaliser. Once you get laughing, everyone is on the same level playing field.

That's why humour is great for business. When you use it effectively you can build trust and rapport faster with your audience. Think about it, if you have a very "technical" element to your message that intimidates people, bringing a bit of humour into the equation to explain things in a non-threatening, funny way can break down the barriers and get people to open up. It can help you explain complicated messages more easily and effectively to gain a higher level of understanding as you are both "speaking the same language."

It's also really useful for changing the energy in a room and getting people focussed again, like combatting the dreaded "straight after lunch slump."

What can you do if you are simply not funny?

The good news is that EVERYONE can be funny!

Unlike an astronaut or a doctor or anything else where you need qualifications, there's no diploma, no job, no degree that you need first in order to be funny!

And I think that's where people struggle with the concept a bit — if you have teaching degree then you are a teacher, or if you have a business then you are a business owner, but there's nothing you can actually get to prove that you are funny. If you look at the flip side of that argument, there's nothing you can get to say that you aren't funny either — so just use that to your advantage!

If you have you ever, ever, ever, ever in your life made someone laugh — even yourself then… Congratulations — you're funny!

The fact is anyone can be funny. You just have to step up to the plate and claim the title!

So now that we have that sorted, the question you should ask is: "How can I be funny more often without it being a hit and miss affair?"

Is there a secret formula to being funny?

I think there's a secret formula to being funny and it involves three steps. Of course, there are technical aspects to learn but the essence is this:

> Step 1. Know yourself and be yourself
>
> Step 2: Know your audience
>
> Step 3: Hold up a mirror to the lives of your audience and point out the truth in a humorous way.

How do you be funny without being cringe worthy?

First up — Be yourself!

Be yourself and being funny will appear effortless and genuine. If you try and be someone else, you'll show up on people's bullsh#* radar and they will run for the hills! Just like a toupee, if there is anything about you that isn't 100% you, it's not the genuine article and it's not believable ... to yourself or your audience!

So how do you be yourself?

First you have to know yourself and we're talking in the communication sense here — for example, do you use short sentences and get to the point or do you like to tell stories? Are you upbeat or deadpan serious? A bit kooky or gentle and nurturing? Are you creative and visual or analytical and wordy?

Play up to your personality and who you naturally are — put that on steroids.

The good news is that all styles work — you just have to own it!

Think about Billy Connolly. He's loud, a bit crazy, swears a lot and moves around the stage lots. Or consider Rowan Atkinson (Mr. Bean) — he's nervous, twitchy, very quiet and hardly ever says anything. Have a look at Jerry Seinfeld — he's almost smug, sarcastic, confident and very laid-back. All very funny people who 100% OWN their style. They know their styles; they don't try to be anyone else. In fact, being themselves is what makes them funny.

So, to be funny you don't need the stereotypical "big nose, plastic moustache glasses" and smoke a cigar going *wakka wakka wakka*! Once you've worked out who you are, just play up your strengths. Put your personality on steroids, and make it an extension of your personality or "supercharged you."

What you do from there is get any sort of information and put it through your personal filter — do things from your point of view with your spin on it and your personality.... Because that is where your funny voice is!

Play up to your personality and who you naturally are — put that on steroids.

If you are in Corporate or Business, how can you be funny and still be taken seriously?

Know your audience! It's crucial to know your audience so that your humour is appropriate and relatable to them so *they* find it funny.

Funny is in the truth. When you hold up a mirror to your audiences lives and point stuff out to them, they will find it funny. If you have no idea who your audience is, then you can't relate to them. You want to know your audience inside out — what they do, what they experience, what they have and so forth.

Find a common ground between you and your audience that you can use for the basis of being funny. If it relates to parts of their life that relate directly to your business, product, service or message even better

It's also a good idea to get really clear on the outcome or purpose when using funny in certain situations to ensure your actions are purposeful and meaningful.

Have a think before you start about what you are trying to achieve. Don't just be funny for the sake of it. Do you want to build trust and rapport quickly, lighten up a boring but essential topic, or do you want to communicate a complicated message in a non-threatening, less confusing way?

A word of caution: It's important to understand that humour should be used to highlight your message not overshadow it. Funny should be used like a spice — too much and it's terrible, not enough and you can't tell it's there, and just the right amount and it's brilliant! Pay attention to how much humour is put into the mix so that you can still be credible.

How do you know if they are laughing with you or at you?

They are laughing with you if they agree with the truth of what you are saying. They are laughing at you if you are totally out of alignment with the real world.

In other words, if you're bonding with people, finding common experiences to share and there's an element of truth that it is inclusive, people will laugh and they'll share that laugh with you.

If you are focusing on the negative side of things, excluding people based on racism, misogyny, abuse, religious or cultural differences just to get a cheap laugh, that's not going to work. That's when people begin to laugh at you or even worse, they ignore your message.

And most importantly DO NOT cross the hurt line!

What's the Hurt line?

It's a term we use in the industry to explain a line in the sand when you've gone too far. When you cross it, you are probably taking cheap shots at people and excluding specific groups and majorly offending someone. Be careful of offensive words and topics, stuff like abuse, misogyny, racism etc. With my work I aim to "do no harm." I want people to feel better after hearing me, not worse.

There's a saying that once you know the rules you can break them. If you ever want to break this rule — this is how you do it… (This is very secret stuff here so make sure you use it with extreme caution and care).

Ok, listen up. If you make it personal and relatable to your own experience you can get away with lots more because you're telling a story of your life instead of making generalised sweeping statements about specific demographic groups.

For instance, a statement like "*all* mums are crazy because…" would cross the hurt line for some women. Even if it was true (it's not — I'm a Mum I should know LOL!), it's much safer to say "*my* mum is crazy because…" Of course, you should probably clear it with the person you're mentioning, but this tip should save you getting into lots of hot water!

Do you suffer from nerves and how do you deal with them?

I used to get extremely nervous before a gig until someone told me that when you get nervous all the blood rushes away from your brain into your muscles to get ready for the "fight or flight" response. When that happens you can't think as well and you forget your lines, and that made perfect sense to me!

It's the same fight or flight mechanism that kicks in during an argument. Later you think to yourself, "oh, I should've said that!" That thought is an indication that the blood has returned back to your brain for normal function!

So now if I feel nervous I focus on getting the blood back to my brain. I do some deep breathing to relax me and then some "anchoring" that I adapted from an NLP seminar to get me into a peak state where I'm fired up, confident and 100% focussed on giving my audience an amazing experience.

How do you practice for a funny presentation?

When rehearsing your presentation, if you have included a funny bit or a joke, it's really important to practice the pacing as though people won't laugh.

The reason for this is if you have practiced pausing for the laughter and when you do the presentation you get "crickets" (silence) then your timing will be all thrown out. If you hit that part in your presentation and it gets a laugh, it's much easier to pause for the laughter than keep going after an unexpected silence.

Give the funny bit of your presentation to the audience as a gift. Don't expect that they'll get the joke, don't expect laughter, just give it from the goodness of your heart... and if they laugh it's a bonus! Never, ever, ever comment that you are making jokes and that they should be laughing — YOU WILL LOOK LIKE AN IDIOT and the audience is almost guaranteed to turn against you!

When you do a presentation, how do you stop the crowd staring at you like you are on TV?

Don't be the lift!

Think about how many times in your life you have been in an elevator/lift. How many of them do you remember? How exciting or engaging were they? I bet most times you just go through the motions and stare into space don't you!

If you are just going through the motions as a presenter, you'll be the lift and the crowd will probably just stare at you. So don't be the lift!

Well that might be all good and well, but how on earth do I do "not be the lift"? I hear you ask!

Try to remember a time when you told someone about a time in a lift. I can think of one time an elderly gentleman in a gopher pinned me to the back wall of the lift when he sped up instead of putting on the breaks. I told that story to everyone!

Now think about why you told people of that time in the lift. I told everyone because I was super angry that this old guy squashed me against the wall and couldn't work out how to reverse so I was pinned there for three floors. It was also out of the ordinary and completely unexpected. We weren't "going through the motions" at all that day!

So the moral of the story is: if you want people to engage and stop staring into space when you are presenting, you need to invoke an extreme emotional response and make it unexpected.

Obviously you don't want that emotion to be directed at you (like boredom or indifference) so they fall asleep or bag you to their friends. You want it to be an extreme emotional response linked with your message or cause and, when that emotional response is unexpected, you will get their attention and stop them staring at you. Obviously I have a background in giving people extreme emotional responses with fun and laughter, but it can be just as effective using emotions of love, hope, joy, anger and sadness.

Any last tips?

There's a saying in the finance industry that money is a magnifier. It's also true with humour and comedy...

Being funny is a magnifier. If you are nice you'll look extra nice, if you are an idiot you'll look like a bigger idiot.

Have fun!

Kristy Moore

Kristy Moore

You're already a speaker

Kristy started out as a caring but shy small-town kid and grew into a citizen of the world. She believes travel and volunteering (locally and globally) are the most amazing ways to open your eyes to new perspectives and understand what really matters to you.

Like many of her childhood friends she took the conventional route of relocating to the city for university, did well in her studies, landed a good job, worked hard and progressed quickly up the corporate ladder. Until she realised that was not the only way to succeed in life.

Kristy had a nagging desire to do something different. On the side of her busy corporate job she volunteered for an Australian children's charity supporting families and brightening their lives when they need it most. In 2011 she volunteered in an impoverished Bolivian children's hospital — an experience that gave her a huge dose of perspective plus the courage to step beyond her everyday comfort zones to pursue her dream of doing work that makes a real difference.

Now, she combines her strong corporate background with her passions for travel and volunteering. She loves making it easier for Australian families and business/corporate teams to get involved in the one thing that was a catalyst for positive change in her own life — sustainable volunteer travel experiences, with peace of mind that their contribution will be lasting.

Kristy's personal mission is to positively change the way people look at life, work and family through travel and volunteering. She is especially passionate about empowering working mothers to enjoy freedom and fulfillment in their everyday lives and be proud role models for their families and teams — both mothers in developing communities overseas and in Australia.

She loves adventurous, ethical world travel, spreading smiles through volunteering, being active outdoors and adding variety to everyday life. She has walked with lions, dived 30 meters below sea level and hiked 4700 meters into the clouds. She thrives on positivity, pursuing big goals and altruistic conversations over a healthy home-cooked meal.

Kristy resides in Melbourne but calls the world her home.

What do you believe are the top 5 attributes of a successful speaker?

1. Being clear on your core message

2. Developing a mindset of delivering your message from a place of service to others

3. Being willing to speak to audiences even when you don't feel ready

4. Being inspirational rather than persuasive

5. Always including a compelling call to action so audiences walk away inspired and actually do at least one thing with the message you've presented

What are your pre-presentation rituals?

Before a presentation, I think about the ideal end result. Not the end of a great presentation or even the end of a confirmed booking for an offering mentioned in the presentation. I think about the longer-term positive impact that my message can have on the lives of other people — people who may not even be in the audience.

For my work-related talks I think about the mother I've helped by sharing my messages. I think about the incredible experience that her family shared on their international volunteer adventure.

I think about welcoming her back to Australia after what she describes as "the best trip of my life — the most wonderful family bonding experience." I think about how grateful she is to have had the opportunity to share this gift with her children and how grateful her children are for the education and opportunities they have. I think about how proud she is of what they achieved together. I think about how happy she is that her whole family has returned safely to Australia with their eyes opened to new perspectives and new possibilities. I think about her new belief that she really can achieve anything she wants.

I also think about the remarkable mothers in rural Kenya and India, knowing that they welcomed this Australian family warmly. I think about the lessons they taught this Australian mother about what's really possible in life, work and family. I think about how far these Kenyan and Indian communities have come from their life of poverty to a life filled with joy knowing their children are free to get the education they missed out on.

 If you have ever felt you're not a naturally talented public speaker, you are not alone

How did you build your confidence as a speaker?

I decided that I had a message worth sharing and that speaking was a great way to spread that message further.

The biggest challenge with building confidence was my mindset of not being a 'naturally' talented public speaker. So many people feel that way about speaking and so many wonderful messages go untold as a result. If you have ever felt this way, then I can confidently say: you are not alone. For me, the biggest breakthrough for overcoming that mindset was to think of speaking as a service to others — if I didn't find a way to overcome my speaking fears and share my message, then people would miss out on what I believe to be incredible opportunities, even life changing.

The other thing that dramatically increased my confidence as a speaker, and is integral to the speaking I do today, is to frame my message around a story. We are all natural storytellers. I find storytelling to be more engaging and memorable for audiences. Stories are also far more enjoyable to prepare and deliver as a speaker, and that passion shines through. After a corporate career of enduring (and delivering) a few too many death-by-PowerPoint presentations, using storytelling in my presentations has dramatically improved my confidence as a speaker.

Do you have a product, program or other offering that you present for sale at speaking events? Do you recommend this for new speakers?

For all speaking events, it's important to have a primary purpose for any presentation. Whether that includes informing people of your offerings really depends on the event. I believe you should include a call to action or next step for your audience, but that doesn't necessarily have to be a product or program.

I host and speak at a number of events specifically focussed on informing families and teams about the experiences they'll have on Hand Up Australia's volunteer travel programs — so the offering is the primary focus of these talks.

As a guest speaker, I may be invited to share our programs or as part of a larger event with multiple speakers. For any event I focus primarily on providing value through information and/or inspiration that will help audience members, regardless of whether offerings are mentioned, taken up or not.

I recommend checking with the event organisers whether it's appropriate for you to share your product, program or other offerings and whether the audience is likely to include people in your ideal target market. If you're not offering something specific, you can still challenge your audiences to take action on one thing they've learned or one idea your talk sparked.

What business are you in and what service does it offer?

I positively change the way people look at their life, work and family through travel and volunteering.

I believe travel and volunteering are the most amazing ways to open your eyes to new perspectives and to really see what's important in your own life. I'm excited and proud to combine my strong business background with my passion for travel and volunteering, with social enterprise, Hand Up Australia. I connect Australian leaders and parents to high-impact and meaningful travel experiences that change lives — theirs, their team/family's and the Indian and Kenyan communities that they provide a hand up to.

For families it's a unique bonding experience with an opportunity to build your legacy and teach your children values of global citizenship, gratitude and community.

For business groups these programs are a stand out way to foster corporate culture, attract and incentivise the right people and connect your brand with an engaged community of Australian youth — our future leaders.

Did you always know the career path you wanted to take? If not, where did you start from and how did you make the change?

Absolutely not! In some ways I led a double life for 9 years. I had a successful (but stressful) corporate consulting career marching from one high-end client to the next, working long hours, wearing dark city suits. I also volunteered for a children's charity in my 'spare time', brightening the lives of families who needed more smiles, wearing bright purple and yellow t-shirts. Both my initial career and my (ongoing) volunteering were great experiences, but I wanted my work to contribute as much fulfillment to others as my volunteer role.

On an overseas volunteer trip, I decided to transition out of the corporate workforce and into social enterprise. Now, with both work and play, I'm contributing to things that make a lasting positive difference and I work to my core strengths, values and interests.

My initial overseas volunteer experience didn't necessarily 'change' me and certainly wasn't the reason for my seemingly rapid career switch. That would have happened eventually. Volunteering internationally opened my eyes to bigger possibilities. It became a turning point for me to re-prioritise my everyday life and focus on what really matters — in life, work and family.

What do you believe was your biggest sacrifice in getting the business off the ground?

Being willing to work for free in the short-term. Whether you work for free or not, you ideally want to love what you do for work or business so much that you are willing to give away your services and to do it with a smile on your face.

That's not to say there won't be challenges (big and small) that will test that smile, but you want to feel like you are continually progressing and that you believe in the bigger picture that your work is contributing to.

Did you have to change your mindset surrounding public speaking? If so, how did you do it?

Absolutely! For years I thought I simply wasn't a natural born speaker and that was it. I certainly wasn't at the point that I refused to present. I put my hand up to deliver training, workshops and presentations, but I felt nervous and uncomfortable if I didn't know exactly what I would say. So I over-prepared and attempted to memorise the words, every single one of them — even for the speeches I did back in high school.

If I knew my content really, really, really well, I was often told I spoke well, but I struggled to accept those compliments due to self-doubt around my speaking abilities.

My mindset shift involved realising that I already had important messages I wanted to passionately share, and I wanted to share that with many more people. That takes a lot of time and energy to do one-on-one, so speaking to larger groups is a more effective way to get my messages out to the world.

After deciding I needed to do more public speaking, I achieved a mindset switch by focusing the audience and the cause or message. It's not about me as a speaker, it's about them. It's also not simply about knowing the content well — it's about wholeheartedly believing in the message or the bigger picture. When I speak about something I'm passionate about, I'm confident that the right people will find it fascinating.

Do you continue to practice your personal development even now?

Yes, and the more I invest in my personal development, the more I achieve in life and work for myself and others. I rarely watch or read mainstream news. Instead, I spend the extra time working on a big goal or reading books/blogs or listen to audios for inspiration. Inspiration is a great start, but it's short lived without action so I like to write a few notes and then take at least one action for my own personal growth.

I also invest in coaching, which has been both my best and worst business investments — I've learnt the importance finding someone that is a good fit for me and that different coaches are needed at different stages or different areas of life and business. Simply taking regular small steps can create pretty incredible developments.

Is there a specific quote or saying that you live by?

"Be the change you wish to see in the world" – Mahatma Gandhi.

This has been a stand out quote for my personal life for many years and I believe it's really important to live it. If we want something changed, the best place to start that change is with ourselves. This quote is now at the forefront of my life *and* the businesses I'm involved in. Hand Up Australia's tagline is Travel | Volunteer | Be the Change, and my personal website's is 'Now Be the Change.' I even have a 'Be the Change' t-shirt!

Through social enterprise, local/global volunteering and everyday actions, I love the journey of being the change I wish to see in our abundant world.

If you could give just one piece of advice about speaking that would make the biggest difference in one person's life, what would that be?

You are already a speaker. People already enjoy listening to you speak. There's a topic, format and audience that's just right for you and they're waiting to hear you speak.

Look at your week so far and the number of conversations you have already had. How did you feel speaking to big and small groups? What sort of topics did you get passionate talking about? Do you prefer long or short discussions? Do you enjoy answering questions that people ask or are you best when you simply stand and deliver your message?

Choose an audience you already feel comfortable speaking to and a topic you already feel comfortable talking about. If that's enough to get your message out, then congratulations and keep going. If you want to step up, start with what you already feel comfortable doing then think about ways you can gradually step beyond that comfort zone either to bigger audiences, different topics or new speaking formats. The world is waiting to hear your voice.

You are already a speaker.

What do you believe are the essential qualities or personal attributes of a successful person?

People define success in many different ways. The first thing I recommend is defining your own success for you. Whatever success means to you, I believe essential qualities and attributes to achieve that success are:

- Knowing your big picture goal and why it's really important

- Building a strong self-belief (it will be tested again and again)

- Putting yourself and your message out for others to hear, even if you don't feel ready

- Accepting that you don't have to have it all figured out

- Trusting that you will figure it out as you go and you will connect with people who can help

- Being grateful for the little successes and lessons along the way

- Persisting — continually putting one foot in front of the other

- Being willing to bounce forward (not back) from setbacks

- Maintaining a mindset of service to others.

What can people do to stay on track, especially when times get tough?

Keep moving and keep believing. If you keep moving forward (even baby steps) and keep believing (in your abilities, why you're doing what you're doing and that you'll find a way to make your big vision happen), then you will be amazed at what you're able to achieve.

What is the most important piece of advice anyone has given you?

Follow your heart. Getting good results in school, going to university, getting a good job, working hard and progressing up the corporate ladder is one way — but it's not the only way. Having done that at the outset and then transitioned to a completely new career, I believe it's important to do work that fulfills you and the people you help.

Lara Shannon

Lara Shannon

It takes confidence in yourself

After a successful advertising and PR career, Lara decided she wanted to try to 'save the world' and has been working as an environmental and social campaigner and media spokesperson for many Australian and UK environmental causes ever since, including the World Wide Fund for Nature (WWF), Planet Ark, Keep Australia Beautiful and many others.

She has presented regular guest environment segments on children's TV shows including Cheez TV, Saturday Disney and Totally Wild and has hosted a wide range of corporate videos, events and awards presentations over the years.

In 2012, Lara launched Ecochick.com to provide a resource and inspiration for people to reduce their environmental footprint through simple, sustainable lifestyle changes. Featuring a blog, eco product reviews and offers, environmental news and much more, Ecochick.com aims to help individuals reduce their impact on the environment in a simple and sustainable way.

Lara is also Host of Eco TV (ecotv.com.au) and has worked as a part-time model and actor over the past 20 years, appearing in numerous TV commercials and shows and a wide range of print ad campaigns.

She also runs a Melbourne-based specialist environment and social change communications consultancy and works as a freelance writer on a range of environmental issues.

From food to fashion and everything in between, Lara is a down-to-earth and inspiring advocate for living life positively. In her spare time, she enjoys walking her dog Max, which in late 2013 prompted her to launch a dog walking business, Puppies at Play.

What do you believe it takes to be a professional speaker?

Having a passion for or deep interest in the topic you are speaking about. Research, getting a broad understanding of the topic and trying to understand how a wide range of people might think about it (i.e. would they agree with your stance or have opposing views?), and then addressing all sides of the argument ensures your presentation is well thought out and well rounded.

It takes confidence in yourself, your knowledge and your ability to be a strong and engaging speaker who keeps your audience entertained and engaged.

What do you believe are the top 5 attributes of a successful speaker?

1. Passion

2. Knowledge

3. Confidence

4. Warmth

5. Humour.

How did you get your first gig, who was it with and what was the experience like?

I worked at the World Wide Fund for Nature (WWF) in my early twenties on a fundraising event selling tickets to the premiere of *Fly Away Home* starring Anna Paquin, Jeff Daniels and Dana Delany.

I was asked to introduce the movie to an audience of 300+ people and talk about issues relating to animal migration. While I was nervous about talking to such a large audience, once I was in front of them with the microphone in my hand I felt quite exhilarated.

In fact, I was able to talk easily because I felt very strongly about helping others learn about important conservation issues. I was also very passionate about my work at WWF so I found it quite easy to speak about the animals and encourage the audience to support our work. I remember how quickly my five-minute talk went — I could have talked for so much longer!

Not long after I did an intro for the launch of another movie — *Africa's Elephant Kingdom* — in Sydney, Melbourne and Adelaide IMAX theatres. I then knew this was what I wanted to keep on doing.

Did you always know the career path you wanted to take? If not, where did you start from and how did you make the change?

At high school I knew I wanted a job that involved writing, acting and presenting. I originally wanted to study journalism but didn't want to restrict myself so I opted for a Bachelor of Arts in Communications Studies, and also studied a Certificate in Advertising and Certificate in Public Relations.

I'd always enjoyed drama at school, so I started working part-time as a model and actor after school. I did audition for a TV reporter's role and also a weather presenter's role while at university, but must admit my confidence and presenting ability was pretty raw at the time. I was fortunate to get a part-time job as a radio producer with a local radio station and also worked for a media monitoring company, so that was how my media career took off.

I was also fortunate to be selected as a Media Marshall for the Queen's Royal Tour to Adelaide in 1992. It was exciting to meet and work for

Queen and Prince Phillip just out of university and it cemented my desire to work a bit outside the box.

However, it was really my desire to help save endangered animals that made me give up media and advertising and take on a corporate fundraising role. Little did I know this move would actually bring all of my skills together and enable me to present a lot more. Having the skills to present allowed me to become a media spokesperson for the environmental charities I worked for and the rest, as they say, is history!

What business are you in and what services does it offer?

I have a few facets to my business these days. I provide public relations and marketing consultancy services to clients, specialising in environmental campaigns and social change causes. This includes copywriting, media release distribution and liaison, advertising campaign advice, sponsorship and events, as well as production and presenter services for corporate videos and TV ads.

Through my website (ecochick.com), I provide environmental, fair-trade and ethical products and services with a promotional platform via product reviews, a newsroom, directory listings and banner advertising.

Who was your first mentor or inspiration?   Was it in person or through books/CDs/seminars?

I've read a lot of the well-known motivational speaker books over the years, not always finishing them, but taking a lot out of them. The two that stick out most are John DeMartini's *Breakthrough Experience* and Tony Robbins' *Awaken the Giant Within*.

I have to admit I was not big on the hard sell at a Tony Robbins weekend workshop I attended — I actually left a day early. However, I remember being extremely in awe of his opening night and how powerful he was on stage. In fact, he was so empowering that when we had to walk over hot coals on that first night I didn't even have to chant, focus my breathing or eye line as we were instructed. He had already instilled me with 100% confidence that walking over coals was easy.

I remember walking away from that weekend thinking what an amazing package Robbins had put together. His presentation had included facts, music, excitement and his confidence was truly inspiring, even though it got a little to 'woo woo' for me after that.

Who are the other mentors that have inspired you? What important lessons have you learnt from them? And do you have a mentor today? If so, who is it and why?

Most recently I went to a networking breakfast featuring the American speaker, Kurek Ashley. I didn't know who he was or what he was going to speak about.

He blew me away. He started telling a story about his days working as an actor on big Hollywood action movies and providing some amazing case studies about the people he'd trained and worked with and how he got them achieving 100% success. I was hanging onto every word he said.

Why? Because he was a living example of his own success and totally believed in himself. I still strive to follow his advice today. His book, *How Would Love Respond* is definitely worth a read and has some great messages for living a successful life (beyond just financial success, too).

Do you continue to practice your personal development even now?

Yes, every day I try to practice personal development in some way, whether it's reading a positive or inspirational book (I have a minimum of five sitting next to my bed I flick through randomly), reading a positive affirmation or reminding myself to live in the moment as often as I can.

I try to attend seminars or networking events to watch what other speakers do. It motivates me when I'm feeling a bit ho-hum. I also have a couple of inspiring life coaches as friends so I attend their workshops and often flick through the notes I've made when I need a bit of a boost.

What is the first step that someone could take if they decided to follow in your footsteps today?

Find what you are passionate about then figure out how you can incorporate it into your work life. Try to work out how can you earn an income from doing what you love or working on a cause that's important to you and has a positive impact on those around you and the wider community. Develop the tools and resources that help you bring your passion to life.

What does success mean to you and how does one achieve it?

To me success means being able to do what you love and either make money from it or have the resources to be able to do it without too much sacrifice.

It isn't about having the best house, car or possessions. It's about being able to work for myself from home and not be part of the rat race. I work long hours — sometimes too long — but I balance this with being able to sleep in if I need to or walk the dogs during the day time when the sun's shining.

Success is also about having a good work/life balance, which can be hard to achieve when workloads are busy. The key is to cultivate the ability to switch off and just enjoy the fun moments without too much thought about what's next or what you have to do tomorrow. If you keep trying to enjoy the simple things in life, spend time laughing with friends and family and do more than just worry about work and money — that's true success.

> *Cultivate the ability to switch off and just enjoy the fun moments without too much thought about what's next or what you have to do tomorrow.*

What keeps you from retiring and lying on the beach every day?

My mortgage! Actually, at the time of writing I'm addressing this by downsizing. However, even if I didn't have to work, I'd still work on ecochick.com and present wildlife and other socially conscious documentaries. I believe in constantly trying to educate people — there's so much more to life than just money and consumption. We should all nourish the planet and society, leaving the world better for having been part of it.

Do you buy lottery tickets? Why or why not?

No — you make your own luck and the only way to fortune is by hard work — that is, if you define fortune in the financial sense.

For me, money isn't the true sign of wealth. Having a happy and fulfilled life, loving and being loved by friends and family — that's what I consider hitting the jackpot. With a one in 45 million chance of winning Oz Lotto, the odds really don't stack up. Not to mention that 70% of lottery winners go broke. I'd rather spend the cost of the ticket on a nice glass of red wine!

Leigh-Chantelle

Leigh-Chantelle

The only way to be a speaker is to speak

Leigh-Chantelle was made in Africa, born in Perth, lived the first ten years of her life on Bougainville Island, Papua New Guinea and now lives mostly in Brisbane, Australia.

She is a published author, international speaker and blogger and runs the online vegan community Viva la Vegan! and not-for-profit, environmental Green Earth Group. She also coordinates in-person and online coaching for Online Etiquette Education, Engaging Volunteers, Staging Effective Events and Effective Activism.

Leigh-Chantelle is an accredited naturopath, nutritionist and Western herbalist who combines her passion for vegan health with natural therapies and healing skills. She has released three Viva la Vegan! recipe calendars, a plant-based Detox Diet e-book, various other recipe e-books and has published many other print books.

Over the past 16 years she has been involved as a sponsor, performer, speaker, MC and stallholder for various animal rights, vegan, vegetarian, environmental and cruelty-free fundraisers, forums, conferences, festivals and events throughout Australia and internationally.

What do you believe it takes to be a professional speaker?

To be professional in any field you have to study, train and go out and use your skills. For a professional speaker, you need to study everything you can about speaking and then get out and do it. Be open to suggestions and ideas from other people, always. If all else fails, fake it until you make it. The only way to be a speaker is to speak.

How do you prepare for a presentation, do you have a specific method you follow and if so what is it?

I write down everything I want to say — it's archaic, but I still use pen and paper — and read everything though. I change anything that doesn't flow or isn't necessary. Then I condense the whole speech into dot points.

I always include at least two quotes that relate to the topic I'm speaking about. I may or may not use a visual presentation to go along with my speech. I always get enough sleep the night before. I do a few vocal warm up exercises — especially humming — and drink lemon and ginger tea before, during and after if possible. I will normally eat and then relax after the talk.

What do you believe are the top 5 attributes of a successful speaker?

I think entrepreneur turned academic, Vivek Wadhwa, says it best: "Speak fearlessly from the heart, get to the point immediately, keep the message simple and focussed, and use the fewest words [you] can." I would also add to know your topic mighty well, inside and out, back to front.

"Speak fearlessly from the heart, get to the point immediately, keep the message simple and focussed, and use the fewest words [you] can."

What's your advice for a new and emerging speaker to find 'guest' speaker spots?

Just ask people if they need speakers.

I know so many people who wait to be asked. Nothing ever happens for me or to me without me making the effort to make these things happen. Not many people will get asked to speak before they're known as a speaker. Therefore, find all the different events in your field in which you'd be interested in speaking, contact the organisers and ask if they have a spot for you.

The worst they can say is 'no.'

Did you always know the career path you wanted to take? If not, where did you start from and how did you make the change?

I grew up wanting to be a rock star but soon realised that the music industry was a lot harder than I thought it would be.

Once I moved away from this very self-involved industry I began to care about things outside of myself — animal rights, feminism, environmentalism, politics. I studied naturopathy, nutrition and Western herbal medicine. When I graduated, I released vegan recipe calendars encouraging people to heal themselves with food. This has evolved over the last eight years to become an interactive, multimedia online community for vegans, vivalavegan.net. I was asked to speak about veganism, animal rights and activism and have travelled internationally to share my knowledge.

I've run a not-for-profit environmental awareness group in Brisbane, Australia since 2009 called Green Earth Group and I've organised, run and marketed large festivals and various smaller events. This led me to speak about staging effective events, teamwork and engaging volunteers. I also run a social media marketing and coaching company so I give talks about online etiquette and social media.

What is your approach to marketing and how did you get your name out into the marketplace?

I'm on top of all the popular social media platforms — from Facebook and Twitter, Pinterest and YouTube to Google+. I focus on creating shareable regular content for my businesses and my clients. This is at least a 6-month plan — some even say 3 years.

Do you recall making a conscious decision to be a speaker? If so, when was it and why?

Originally I started out speaking only when someone asked me to and I've developed my talks from there.

When I was at one speaking event about four years ago, a corporate speaker friend said I should focus on speaking as a profession, particularly in the corporate world. I had never thought of it before then. He said only about 1% of the population are comfortable and enjoy public speaking and I should capitalise on that.

After the seed was planted, I focussed on refining my skills and speeches. I worked on a couple of things he suggested and have added "speaker" and "coach" to my CV.

What have you found are the best methods or strategies for keeping motivated and focussed?

I love lists, timetables, timelines, quotes and I'm very goal-focussed. I surround myself with positive and empowering people who are on the same life path as me. I have various lists of my daily, weekly and monthly goals and am in the process of achieving my yearly ones. I've always been a self-motivator and I find if I start the day off with exercise — laps in the pool, yoga or Pilates — and eat a well-balanced vegan diet I'm always ahead of the game mentally and physically.

 I've always been a self-motivator and I find if I start the day off with exercise — laps in the pool, yoga or Pilates — and eat a well-balanced vegan diet I'm always ahead of the game mentally and physically.

Is there a significant quote or saying that you live by?

"Your choices matter,

Your actions make a difference,

Your example will influence others."

This was something I received from the universe when doing a tarot reading for myself and it's helped me a lot over the years.

What is the first step that someone could take if they decided to follow in your footsteps today?

Stop talking and start walking. I'm a mentor and massive supporter for those who help themselves. The best way to learn is to get out there and do something — you will definitely make mistakes, but as long as you learn from them and stay focussed you will achieve your goals.

Stop talking and start walking.

In your opinion, is it harder for women to create significant wealth?

Women are still paid less, have less savings and superannuation, have more time off from work and put other things ahead of earning money. I think — and I speak for myself here as well — that women need to focus more on their careers and goals to set themselves up financially. A partner or a husband isn't a financial security — especially with over half of marriages ending in divorce. It's time we all take responsibility for our action (or inaction) now and change the course of our futures.

What is the worst thing that has ever happened to you during a speaking engagement and how did you recover your equilibrium to continue?

Three of us were speaking in an hour-long segment. One of our members wasn't around to speak to, so we moved their speech to last.

The first person spoke for 15 minutes with five minutes for questions and then I got up to speak. I walked to the podium and started. The missing person came right up the front to one of the organisers and — next to the video camera filming my talk — launched into a tirade about the conference, the organiser and about me speaking.

I was shocked but ignored this disrespectful person and kept talking. One of the organisers then gave me a five-minute warning just when I was starting to get into the main part of my talk. I was a bit ruffled, but paused with a deep breath and said, "I've just been advised I only have five minutes now when I was to talk for longer, so if you have any questions or comments please see me later or see some similar videos on YouTube."

I finished my talk and left the room still composed. I had a bit of a rant to a friend I ran into later and went out of my way to thank the organisers again for putting on the event. I can't stand rude people — no matter who they are or who they think they are.

Lisa Page

Lisa Page

Just do what you love

Lisa was born in South Australia in 1972, where she lived until she was 19. Since then, she's spent most of her adult life living and working overseas in Europe, Asia, New Zealand, USA and the UK.

She is the founder of SoulSatisfactionforWomen.com, a global education business that provides mentoring, coaching, and information products to women and couples.

An international speaker, coach and the author of numerous digital books and programs, including 'Life, Love & Intimacy' and 'Breathe Baby Breathe', for over 20 years, Lisa has been exploring the deeper truths of life, love and intimacy.

And while she enjoyed fabulous success in the corporate world, being placed in the top 20% of female earners in Australia in her early twenties and winning many awards for her fine dining restaurant after, Lisa knew in her heart there was more to this life!

So she ditched it all to dive deep into spiritual inquiry, living in an ashram for three years. Since then, she's been passionately sharing the integral wisdom, cutting-edge research and the powerful tools she discovered to help other women create the success and lifestyle they desire without sacrificing the juice and truth of who they are as a rich, soulful women.

Lisa's qualifications include a Diploma in Dru Yoga Therapy, Masters in Ericksonian Hypnosis, Masters in Neurological Repatterning, Masters in NLP, NLP Trainer and Masters in Performance Coaching. Because she's deeply passionate about living what she teaches, she continues to study for her own personal development with teachers such as best-selling author and sacred intimacy master, David Deida.

Lisa has presented live workshops and seminars in Australia, UK and Europe. She has also delivered online keynote presentations and has featured in radio, magazines and websites with a global audience, reaching thousands of women worldwide. She's the 'go-to' speaker and coach for highly successful women and couples.

Lisa lives by a South Australian beach with her partner and 12-year-old son.

Do you suffer from nerves and if so how do you manage them?

I don't 'suffer from nerves', but of course I do get nervous sometimes. I think that's natural. It's just your nervous system putting you on 'alert.'

I've worked with some of the top speakers from around the world, and I can honestly say that there are very few speakers I've met who *don't* get nervous sometimes. The question is what do you do with your nerves? Do you allow them to paralyse you, or do you use them to bring aliveness to your body and alertness to your mind?

They say that the two greatest fears are death and public speaking.

I think the fear of public speaking essentially comes from the deeply rooted, and very human fear, of humiliation. In fact, people often describe humiliation as worse than death! They say things like, *"I was so humiliated. I just wanted to curl up and die!"*

So if nerves become a real issue for you, it's important to explore what's underneath them. And I do have a technique you can use for that, which I'll share later on.

Nerves, like any 'unwanted' feeling, are a great opportunity for self-exploration. When you notice nerves are taking over, that's the time to explore and let go of the underlying fears that are causing the nerves, such as the fear of being judged, 'getting it wrong', being laughed at, feeling vulnerable, getting heckled, or feeling humiliated.

The reason it's so important to explore and release these fears is because, left unchecked, they prevent you from being fully, and authentically YOU, both on and off stage. And that can profoundly affect your success, the impact you have as a speaker, your relationships and your sense of personal fulfilment.

On the other hand, the more you cultivate your sense of self-worth, the more what you think, feel and do, come into deeper alignment. Then you're much less affected by other people's opinions. You receive what they say with an open heart, but you can discern what is their judgement and what is yours to work on. And with that level of discernment, you're much more able to trust yourself, and trust that some of the audience will love you, some will hate you, and some will think you're OK.

... And that's OK!!!

That feeling of 'OK-ness' no matter what anybody else thinks, makes you naturally more charismatic, and irresistibly magnetic because people *want* to be around people who are authentic, relaxed, passionate, real, and totally comfortable in their own skin.

There's a quote from Brene Brown that I love. She's a best selling author, and a shame and vulnerability researcher. She says that whenever she gets nervous, or can feel tension arising, she simply affirms to herself:

"Don't puff up. Don't shrink back. Just stand your sacred ground."

I love this because it can be so tempting to shrink back when you're scared, or to puff up as a protection mechanism when you don't feel so good about yourself. But when you just stand your sacred ground as a presenter, you give everyone else in the room permission to do the same. And that's a tremendous gift to give anyone, let alone a room full of people!

I was an event manager for a few years working with some of the world's top speakers in London, Europe and Australia where the audiences ranged from 25 to 8000. So I got to see speakers at their best and their worst, at their most confident and their most nervous.

One of the things I noticed was that the speakers who handled their pre-gig nerves well were also good at creatively dealing with the inevitable 'mishaps' that arose during an event. I learned a lot from those speakers, as I watched them from the back of the room, not only handling those situations with ease, but even artfully using the situations as an opportunity to bring their audience into even deeper rapport and trust.

 Speakers who handled their pre-gig nerves well were also good at creatively dealing with the inevitable 'mishaps' that arose during an event.

This formed an invaluable part of my training as a speaker, and came in handy, especially in the early days when one particular day, my nerves did almost get the better of me.

I remember walking onto the platform and, as I looked out at their eagerly awaiting faces, my mouth went dry and my mind went completely blank! So I took a deep breath, welcomed them and got them to close their eyes for a five minute *'get in touch with what really matters to you'* meditation, while I took a few deep breaths myself, grounded my feet into the floor, relaxed my body, opened my heart, and cleared my mind.

Much to my relief, they loved the meditation. And it gave me the time I needed to get myself together. That taught me a lot about thinking creatively on my feet, and trusting myself to get out of sticky situations without the crowd even knowing anything had 'gone wrong'!

So if nerves do hit you on stage.

Don't panic!

There's always a solution.

TIP: If you're a new speaker, then it's good to think about all the things that 'could' go wrong, so you can use the power of your creative thinking and imagination to brainstorm ways to handle them in advance.

It's been scientifically proven that your body doesn't know the difference between 'imagining' and 'doing'. So take some time, to imagine yourself handling those situations really well. Then, if they do happen, you won't panic as much, because your brain and nervous system will 'recall' that you've already handled this situation before, and you're much more likely to be able to think on your feet and come up with a creative solution, instead of going into a blind panic.

It's been scientifically proven that your body doesn't know the difference between 'imagining' and 'doing'. So take some time, to imagine yourself handling those situations really well.

For example, imagine for a moment you're on the stage and someone starts to heckle you.

Imagine all the ways you could confidently and compassionately handle the situation, in a way that quietens the heckler, and keeps the rest of the crowd on side at the same time.

Or imagine what you'd do if the microphone stopped working and the sound went dead, or someone's mobile phone rang at a critical point in your presentation. These are all things, by the way, that will inevitably happen to you at one time or another as a speaker. So mentally preparing yourself will give you an edge as a professional speaker, especially when you're just starting out.

Nerves, like any 'unwanted' feeling, are a great opportunity for self-exploration.

What exercises do you do to relax before a presentation?

Because of my background in yoga, meditation and stress management, I've got a bunch of 'instant calm' techniques up my sleeve to relax before a presentation.

There are three essential techniques that I use to ensure that I'm most relaxed, present and empowered for my presentation. What you'll notice is that all three of these techniques involve using your breath, and that's because how you breathe has a fundamental affect on your nervous system, which in turn instantly changes how you think, how you feel and what you say or do in the moment.

That's why when we have a friend who is in a panic, we instinctively say things like *'It's OK, just breathe."* Or *"Take a deep breath."*

So here are three of my top techniques for staying relaxed on stage:

The first technique is a great way to release any persistent nervousness or worry that you might have about an upcoming gig (or anything else in your life). This technique helps you to access the wisdom beneath the tension, and to use it as an opportunity for personal growth, empowerment and success.

What you do is, take some quiet space where you won't be interrupted, and sit quietly with your spine straight. Take a few deep breaths all the way into your belly until you have good body awareness. Wiggle your toes and feel your feet on the ground as you breathe, if you find it difficult to 'get out of your head'.

Next, begin to notice where you FEEL the nerves or worry in your body. Notice any sensations, such as tension, constriction, heat, cool or whatever it feels like for you in the moment. Choose the strongest sensation to work with first, and with your sternum lifted, breathe fully and allow that sensation to grow to its fullest potential. Just allow it to be as big, as deep, as wide, or as intense as it can be.

Now, holding awareness of that sensation, place your tongue on the roof of your mouth. As you breathe in, travel your awareness down the front surface of your body down to your pelvis, and then as you breathe out, let your awareness naturally move up your spine, all the while still noticing the sensation that belongs to that tension. This is called a breath circulation practice. After a couple of breath circulations, ask yourself, "What do I need to let go of to be free of this tension?"

Feel yourself letting go of whatever it is. Then affirm to yourself "Having released that, I'm now ready to love and trust that I ..." (Fill in the blank with the wisdom that is revealed to you.)

Using the power of your breath, allow that wisdom to permeate every cell of your being. Then repeat the same process with any other threads of tension you notice.

The realisations that will come to you through this practice will be powerful and liberating because you're called to release the fear and reclaim the empowerment that was hiding beneath it.

 As one of my greatest teachers, David Deida says, "Behind your greatest fear is your greatest gift."

The second technique is one that I do right before I go on stage for a presentation. It will help you to relax your body, open your heart, clear your mind and step into your most powerful presence.

Take a quiet moment, and with legs hip width apart, anchor your feet into the ground, like roots of a tree. Feel the support of the earth beneath you. Keep your feet anchored into the earth, and at the same time, raise your awareness up your body until you reach the expanse that exists just above your crown. So now you feel both grounded at your feet, and expanded, in your mind. Lift your sternum gently to ensure your heart is open. With your tongue on the roof of your mouth, do the circulation breath as described above for a few rounds, until you feel ready to go!

The third technique I want to share with you is something I always do when I first step on a stage. This is the best way I know how for you to create instant connection, rapport and trust between you and your audience. It also establishes you as a powerful presence right off the bat, and creates a space for authenticity and an excitement in the crowd for what's next.

When you first step onto the stage, take your time before you speak. Bring yourself into an aligned standing posture with your feet hip width apart, feet firmly anchored into the ground, knees are soft, sternum is slightly lifted and your shoulders are relaxed.

Before you speak, take a couple of full, relaxed breaths. Soften your gaze and allow your vision to expand to include all audience members. You can do this even in a really big auditorium and everyone will feel 'seen' by you. Breathe. Smile. And really drink your audience in through that soft gaze. Allow yourself you really see and feel them and for them to see and feel you.

Now this might seem like an eternity as I write this here, but it only takes a few moments and it's well worth it! Through your body, breath and presence you're essentially saying, *"I'm here for YOU! I know you came to solve a pressing problem and I'm here to do my best to help you with that. I care about you."*

Just remember. After the event, people won't so much remember WHAT you said, but how you made them feel. And that starts from the moment you walk out onto the stage.

What kind of training/development did you undertake to become the speaker you are today?

I've done a few 'official' speaker-training courses over the years with some amazing teachers.

Those trainings have been incredibly helpful to help me to structure and craft my presentations in a way that not only educates and inspires the audience, but also, and most importantly, moves them into meaningful action. This is an essential piece because they come to an event to get a problem solved, but rarely can it be solved without some action on their part. So unless you as a speaker can move your audience into meaningful action, they'll most likely remain stuck in their problem.

Aside from those trainings, as I look back I realise that in all the work I've ever done, both as an employee and as a business owner, I've always done some kind of speaking or training. And that 'real world' experience has really made me the speaker that I am today.

It started when I left home at 19 to work at the World Expo in Seville, Spain with the Australian Government. There I had to speak in front of crowds of five to 300 tourists at a time, inspiring them with facts woven into stories about Australia. I had to speak not just in English but also in the other languages I knew, French, Italian and Spanish! That was a very steep learning curve at a young age, but it taught me a lot.

As I spoke, I saw their eyes light up with excitement and possibility. It was then that I realised that I wasn't just sharing facts and stories about kangaroos, Australian wines and argyle diamonds — I was educating them, inspiring them and opening them to the possibility of new adventures in a far away land. And that's exactly what they came for.

 Don't panic! There's always a solution.

From there I worked with an Australian-based marketing company for 5-Star hotels and resorts in Sydney, New Zealand and South East Asia. My role was not only to recruit 30 local employees in each new location every six months, but also to train them into a cracker sales team.

In South East Asia especially, I'd have to train each new group quite extensively because there were very few 'trained sales people' to hire.

This gave me great practice as a speaker and trainer and, as I look back now, essentially my intention then was the same as it is today: To educate, inspire, and empower each person, to transform their fears into their greatest gifts, both in their work and life.

Even when I moved to the USA and became Director of Member Services at the Beverly Hills Country Club in Los Angeles, I still found myself creating new programs where I would hold events for new members, and training for staff. So each new 'job' I had, added to my speaking expertise and experience.

The same thing happened when I ran my own multi-award winning restaurant in South Australia, and then when I gave it all up to become a yoga and meditation teacher. There I was again, running my own workshops and events around yoga and stress management!

But it was probably my time in London where I worked as an event manager for a large global event company that my training as a speaker took a massive leap. I was fortunate to work with some of the world's top speakers, so while I continued to run my own workshops I also got to experience the power of live events from the back of the room.

With events ranging from 25 to 6000 people, this gave me an in depth understanding of what differentiates a good event from a great event, or a good speaker from one who is absolutely unforgettable!

How did you get your first gig, who was it with and what was the experience like?

My first gig was self-created.

I'm a bit of a 'what if' girl, so straight after my four year Diploma in Dru Yoga Therapy, I thought to myself, *"What if I shared this with the corporate world? What if I shared this with kids with behavioural problem? What if I shared this with women refuges?"* And so it began!

I started running my own workshops and found it easy to do, even before my event management days. I'm a details chick, so with a background in marketing, service and sales I never had a problem filling a room and got immense pleasure out of attending to every little detail to make the experience really special for each audience member.

Most importantly, I've always had a deep belief that what matters most is how the client FEELS from the moment they walk through the door to the moment they leave.

So you've got to be able to 'walk in your audience members shoes.' Get a FEEL for what concerns them? What are they afraid of? What pains them? What do they want to get out of this event with you? Why is it so important to them? It's all about how they FEEL.

People rarely take action, including buying your product based on logic. They buy based on how they feel and then they back it up with logic. So whether your intention is to inspire them to recycle their rubbish, or to buy your product or service because you know it will serve them, you've got to tap in to how they feel… every step of the way.

These days, as the founder of 'Soul Satisfaction for Women,' I've spoken live to audiences in Australia, London and Europe and online to women from all around the world. So I'm living proof that if you love what you do, your heart's in the right place and you're willing to do what it takes, you can go from small events in your local town to speaking on the world's stage.

Do you have a product, program or other offering that you present for sale at speaking events? Do you recommend this for new speakers?

Yes I always have a 'next step' planned for my audience at speaking events.

I'm a big believer that your audience comes to you because they have a problem they want solved. If they knew how to solve it themselves, they wouldn't be at your event. They'd just be getting on with it!

And live events are one of the best ways I know how, to share your message, give great educational value, and inspire people into action, so they can solve the problem they came to you for.

However it's pointless inspiring them to action, if you know they'll need more guidance than you've been able to give at the event. And most events aren't long enough for a complete solution. So that's why offering your 'next step' is so important.

And it's not just about making money at the event. It's about providing a solution that has real value, is a great fit for those who need it and also provides you with rich reward for that solution.

So if ever you feel shy about 'selling'. Ask yourself these questions:

> *"How will my offer help them to solve the problem they have? What pain will it save them? What relief will it give them? How much is that worth to someone who is suffering this problem?"*

Once you know the answer to these questions it's easy to feel good about what you're offering.

In fact, I'd venture to say that if you know you can help them solve a problem and get the result they came to you for, then you're even doing them a disservice by NOT offering them a way forward with you.

What I offer depends on the event type and whether it's my own event where I have free range to offer whatever I like, or a guest speaker event, where I need to comply with my host.

For my own events, I have a range of programs and products that I offer such as live trainings, coaching programs, online digital programs, online mentor programs, and evergreen products".

(**'Evergreen' is a term you use when you run a program, record it to create a digital downloadable product, and then put it on your website where it remains 'evergreen' and can be sold over and over again, making you money while you sleep!)

For guest speaker events, I always find out what I can about the event and the audience prior to the event. Things like:

- Whether it's a free or paid event

- What else will be offered at the event

- What are the key problems the audience is hoping to solve at the event

- Anything else that might be helpful for me to tailor my presentation and offering to that specific audience.

If the host says there's 'no selling' at their event, I still ask if they'd like me to provide their audience with a free gift. They rarely say no to that! And I offer a digital download product, or free webinar series in exchange for their email address. If you do this, it's essential to think about the logistics and plan ahead with the host or event manager so you know you've got your forms ready and printed and a way for them to be handed out, filled in, collected and returned to you.

If the host says yes, this is a win, win, win!!!

A win for the host because they get to look great while they give their audience members even greater value. A win for the audience because they get one step closer to solving the problem they came for. And a win for you because you get to grow your database with qualified leads. These are people who already know, like and trust you because they've experienced you first hand at the event, and by giving you their email address they're essentially confirming that they love what you do and want to know more.

Even if you're just starting out as a speaker, there's always something you can offer an audience. If you're in business you have something to offer!

And when you craft your offer to solve a specific problem and give great value, then you'll not only make good money at your event you'll also cultivate long-term relationships with new people who'll soon become your most loyal clients and raving fans if you treat them right!

The one thing I would say about selling from stage is this. Of course you have sales targets for your events, but I can guarantee from personal experience as an event manager and speaker the audience knows when you're just trying to 'sell' them to meet a sales target. They can feel desperation a mile away and there nothing more off-putting! Gone are the days of high-pressure event sales. People want to feel appreciated and valued. They want their problem solved and they demand value, and rightfully so.

So how you structure your pricing is incredibly important.

You've got to cost it out in a way that delivers all you promise and more, and still richly rewards you in the process. Also, when you announce the price in your offer, it's got to feel like a no-brainer to YOU first. Only then will it feel like a no-brainer to your audience. So make sure you feel totally congruent with your offer and price. Otherwise they'll feel it and it will negatively affect your sales.

Remember, value is in the eye of the beholder. It is determined by how urgent the problem FEELS to the client, how much they FEEL they'll 'get' in return for their investment, and how much they FEEL they can trust you to deliver the solution you've promised.

Did you always know the career path you wanted to take? If not, where did you start from and how did you make the change?

It's funny because when I was a kid I always wanted to be an explorer, a teacher *and* a psychologist. And in a sense I've wound up in a business and a life where I get to do all three!

It's been a journey from where I started to now. I've been a student, a government employee, a marketing manager, a restaurant owner, a yoga and meditation teacher, a stress management consultant, an event manager, a relationship coach, a sacred intimacy teacher... and a few other things in between.

I'm an accumulator by nature. I love to accumulate knowledge, both professionally and personally, live it and then share it. Over the last 20 years I've been exploring the deeper truths of life, love and intimacy and all my work, travel, professional training and my own personal discoveries along the way have brought me to where I am today.

I consider myself an eternal student, which is probably why I'm so drawn to teaching and speaking. I just feel incredibly blessed as an international speaker and coach, that I get to share what I've learned with amazing clients from around the world, doing what I love every single day!

What business are you in and what services does it offer?

As the founder of 'Soul Satisfaction for Women' I feel like I have the best job in the world! I get to run a global education business from my beachfront home that reaches thousands of people worldwide. That in itself is pretty amazing!

For over 12 years now, we've provided both live and online events, mentoring, coaching programs and products that educate, inspire and empower women (and couples) with powerful ways to easily dissolve stress, boost energy, magnify their success, spice up their love life and deepen their sense of personal fulfilment.

And my part in all that is as a speaker, coach and writer where I get to do what I'm most deeply passionate about, which is sharing integral wisdom, profound empowerment practices, cutting edge research and powerful tools in a way that can be applied easily in everyday life.

What is the most important piece of advice anyone has ever given you?

The most important advice I ever got was from my Mum. It's amazing how one comment can stay with you forever and have such a deep impact on your life.

One day, I was in a flap about subject choices for school, and she said:

> "Don't do what everyone else is doing, don't even do what you're good at. Just do what you love!"

So I chose to continue with French, Italian and Spanish, which didn't really make logical sense at the time because I wasn't sure what I'd use them for. But her sage advice definitely paid off because, after two years at university, I got my first job overseas at the tender age of nineteen, in Spain with the Australia Tourist Commission.

And from there I've spent the rest of my life travelling the world, doing what I love, and being richly rewarded for it! Thanks Mum!

What keeps you from retiring and lying on the beach every day?

What keeps me from retiring and lying on the beach every day? Well, probably the fact that I *do* live on the beach and that I *absolutely love* what I do so much, that even if I didn't get paid for it, I'd still be doing it!

So I guess for now I get the best of both worlds!

Do you buy lottery tickets? Why or why not?

No, I've never really been a lottery ticket buyer. Every now and then I might have a flutter if I feel lucky, but my parents raised me to deeply believe in doing what I love, working smart, investing my money to build the financial wealth I want and creating the lifestyle I desire.

My Dad has always been a source of deep inspiration for me because he's a self-made multi-millionaire who decided not to follow in his father's footsteps in the family business because he really wanted to pursue what he was passionate about — cars!

Instead of becoming a publican, he built a thriving automobile business, which is still successful 40 years later!

So I watched him build that business as a young girl and then saw him reach the stage where he could buy his own private airplane, get his pilot's license and take us away on amazing family adventures in the middle of the Simpson Desert or uninhabited islands off the coast of Australia. And then he swapped the plane for boats and a new series of breathtaking sea adventures.

Essentially, he showed me how to build a business you love to support the lifestyle you love. That coupled with my Mum's advice to "...*Just do what you love,*" has had a profound impact on the way I live my life.

Maureen Bell

Focus on your audience

Maureen was born in Glenbrook in the Blue Mountains in 1966. After completing her diploma in Catering Management, she travelled extensively throughout the world for three years working in hotels. Returning to Australia, she joined Flight Centre where her excellent performance saw her progress through the company from store manager to human resources manager at Flight Centre USA.

One of her many career highlights was developing and delivering a national Leadership Training program adopted by Flight Centre across all global operations. It was during this work that Maureen realised any presentation topic can be made interesting when it is delivered with passion and a focus on the audience. She began to identify and develop innovative techniques designed to engage, influence and inspire.

She started working on her own with SMEs focusing on developing and facilitating leadership programs. While coaching she realised how important it was for leaders to being able to present and communicate as well as observing what an enormous hurdle public speaking presented for most leaders.

In 2010, she founded "Speak with Presence," a Sydney-based boutique consultancy that coaches business leaders and executives in the art of delivering phenomenal presentations. With a powerful program drawn from almost two decades of experience, Maureen helps high-performing individuals overcome their fears and stresses in the public arena. It's her mission to help business leaders become great presenters that speak from their voice AND heart — because then they have the power to influence, inspire and motivate others.

Maureen has just published her first book, a step-by-step guide to writing and delivering confident, authentic and engaging presentations. Her work has led to a TV appearance plus various articles in Australian magazines. She regularly speaks on "overcoming public speaking fear to open the door to opportunities."

Maureen now lives in Sydney with her husband and three children.

Do you suffer from nerves and if so how do you manage them?

Yes, I usually do suffer from nerves before a presentation or speaking event. Years of experience have taught me to welcome the nerves because they show you care. When I'm nervous it reminds me to prepare more to ensure I give my audience value.

In the few days leading up to an event I often wake in the middle of the night thinking about my speech. My stomach feels heavy and I feel on edge. To deal with this nervous energy I practice deep or "belly breathing," which takes my body from the fight/flight response to a calmer relaxed and present state.

I prepare my presentation very well and then practice over and over again. I always practice my presentation or speech in the same way I intend to deliver it — standing up, speaking out loud and with my laptop (if showing slides). I imagine there's an audience in my lounge room. These techniques are incredibly effective to manage my nerves leaving me feeling calm and in control.

What exercises do you do to relax before a presentation?

Every time I speak or present I do the following:

- Deep or "belly breathing" **daily** for five minutes, leading up to an event

- Visualisation daily

- Exercise — to expend the nervous energy the morning of the presentation

- Just before I present I have a basic ritual to awaken my body and focus my thoughts. I find a quiet place wherever possible to prepare myself mentally and physically for what I'm about to do for 10 minutes.

It's worth investing time in the above exercises to feel energised, more relaxed and present. You'll be more in tune with what you have to say.

How do you customise your presentation to meet the needs of the audience?

I aim to get to know my audience as best as I can. Firstly, establish their concerns and challenges by answering the following questions:

1. How are they currently thinking?

2. How are they currently feeling?

3. What are they currently doing?

4. After the presentation, what do you want your audience to think, feel and do?

I was once asked to deliver a presentation on *Speaking with Confidence* for a small advertising company. I asked if I could speak beforehand with several of the attendees to really find out how they were thinking, feeling and doing. This ensured I addressed their specific needs rather than making incorrect assumptions. While speaking I recalled specific examples cited by those I spoke to (make sure you get approval first, especially if you name names).

Collate as much information as possible about your audience before your presentation. Consider their feelings, thoughts and current actions and what you want these to be after you present.

If you're focussed on your audience you won't have much time to focus on yourself, so your nerves will be reduced.

Did you always know the career path you wanted to take? If not, where did you start from and how did you make the change?

No, I had no idea I would end up running my own business specialising in presentation skills for business leaders.

Early in my career I was given an opportunity to present to a group of team leaders on goal setting as a result of my success in achieving our monthly targets. I was extremely lucky to have a mentor in the human resources department who showed me how to prepare a presentation and told me to practice, practice, practice and practice again.

This initial presentation kicked started my learning and development career within the company and over the years I progressed from store manager to human resources manager. I really enjoyed speaking and presenting and had many opportunities to do this at conferences, meetings and daily as a facilitator.

As a mother I wanted flexibility and to explore working with other companies. So I founded my own training business, "Bell Learning & Development" in 2002, working with small companies to help them develop and implement sales and leadership training.

During this time I was working with emerging team leaders and kept hearing and experiencing similar stories about leaders who were terrified to speak in public or avoided taking opportunities due to their fear of public speaking.

So in 2010 I created "Speak with Presence," a training business that coaches business leaders and executives in the art of delivering phenomenal presentations. It's now my mission to help business leaders become great presenters who speak from their heart and therefore have the power to change the world.

Looking back, I followed a path I loved, that constantly challenged me and put me out of my comfort zone. As a result I l acquired new skills and grew as a person. My philosophy is do what you love and you will excel.

Did you change your mindset surrounding public speaking? If so, how did you do it?

While I get nervous, I've always enjoyed speaking in front of others and therefore never had a fearful or negative mindset about doing it. However, I did have to change the focus of my public speaking.

The mindset I had to develop was, "it's not about me; it's about the audience." This was a big shift. In the beginning I thought everyone would be interested in everything I had to say. No! In order to keep engaging audiences it's essential to have an audience-focussed mindset. Another way to look at it is to ask, "what's in it for them?" This is now my focus every time I plan a presentation.

In the beginning I thought everyone would be interested in everything I had to say. No! In order to keep engaging audiences it's essential to have an audience-focussed mindset.

Who was your first mentor or inspiration?

When I was facilitating leadership at Flight Centre I was introduced to Patricia Fripp and many other presenters through a program called, "Bullet Proof Manager" (a video-based, live-facilitated management training).

Patricia Fripp is a dynamic and experienced speaker. I loved her message and the engaging way she delivered it. Since then I have followed her work closely. She is part of "Champions Edge," which allows me to connect with six of the best speaker coaches in the world and have access to their insights, skills and techniques.

Is there a significant quote or saying that you live by?

"Watch your thoughts, they become words;

watch your words, they become actions;

watch your actions, they become habits;

watch your habits, they become character;

watch your character, for it becomes your destiny."

Upanishads

Put simply, we are what we think.

If you could give just one piece of advice about speaking that would make the biggest difference in one person's life, what would that be?

Quite often fear will get in the way. People remain silent in meetings, at social occasions or refrain from putting their hands up for speaking opportunities.

Yes, public speaking can be nerve wracking. However, having the courage to move out of your comfort zone and speak in whatever forum is applicable for you creates opportunities. Manage your fear, trust your instincts and take that important first step.

My advice is to forget the nerves and go for it, as the opportunities that come from speaking out are endless.

Manage your fear, trust your instincts and take that important first step.

Mary's Story:

A nurse educator at a large Sydney hospital, Mary decided to submit a paper for an International Nursing Conference. She had just completed a research project on practice development and it was the perfect opportunity to showcase her work. It would also challenge her to be up on the big stage.

As part of her preparation Mary asked for feedback from colleagues. Her professor — a numbers woman — advised: "Don't dumb the presentation down, give the audience facts and figures." A creative person, Mary had wanted to use images as metaphors to get her message across and was quite shattered with this feedback.

Two days before the submission deadline Mary hadn't done a thing. The day before she was too worried about her paper to sleep. She didn't know what to write. But she knew she had to present a paper that was authentic for her.

Then at 3am she sat at her computer, lit a candle and said to herself: "If you weren't afraid, what would you write?"

She typed for three hours. When she was finished she was tired but energised. She knew she'd done a great job.

After the presentation a member of the audience introduced herself. Her name was Angela, the guru of practice development in the UK. "I'm very interested and amazed at how many people put their hand up to participate in the research you conducted," she told Mary. "Could I interview you at lunch time?"

Angela later invited Mary to Oxford University for a weekend to catch up and to see her work. It was a dream come true. And it all happened because she had the guts to deliver a presentation from the heart. Being true to yourself and willing to give something a go is so important.

Angela now provides constructive criticism of Mary's work and they keep in regular contact on Skype. Angela has submitted her name to the editor of a journal she writes for as a possible contributor about her work in Australia.

These opportunities opened up for Mary because she managed her fear, trusted her instincts and took that first step.

As a speaker what is the most common question you get asked and what is your answer.

The most common question I'm asked is how to overcome the fear of public speaking.

Recognise that almost EVERYONE experiences some anxiety or nervous energy when presenting publicly. It's completely normal.

There's no miraculous strategy or technique that will dissolve your fear of public speaking completely. In fact, nerves are good as they drive to prepare thoroughly and avoid complacency. What's important is how you manage your nerves so they work for you, not against you. Research suggests that feeling nervous can help us perform tasks more efficiently and can improve our memory. Good stress is something we want. Good stress stimulates us.

 Avoidance increases the fear. Action decreases it.

My top 10 techniques to manage the fear are:

1. Develop the right mindset that will work for you not against you

2. Know how you are going to start and conclude

3. Be well prepared

4. Practice, practice and keep practicing

5. Prepare a good outline of your notes and refer to these notes while speaking

6. The audience is on your side

7. Deep "belly breathing"

8. Visualisation exercises

9. Arrive early and prepare

10. Welcome your audience upon arrival, if it is possible. This allows you to connect and get to know them before you speak.

What does success mean to you and how does one achieve it?

1. Do what you love — it makes your work life easier

2. Be around the people you care for and love

3. Have financial independence to make choices.

To achieve success you first have to define what you want and then set goals. I set **SMART** goals:

- **S**pecific. They must be specific to you and what you want to achieve

- **M**easurable. They are easily measured and therefore managed

- **A**chievable. A goal must be achievable for *you* and *your* business, not someone else's business

- **R**ealistic. Set a goal that is realistic within your world

- **T**ime. Give all your goals a timeframe so that you know when to reach them.

I then identify how to achieve my goals: what action do I have to take to make them become a reality? The discipline is remaining focussed on what is important to me and working towards achieving only those goals. It's important to have milestones along the way and celebrate them as you go.

I have a board above my desk with pictures of what's important to me. Seeing these each day motivates me and makes me incredibly grateful for what I have.

What is the worst thing that has ever happened to you during a speaking engagement and how did you recover you equilibrium to continue?

I was presenting an interactive two-hour talk to a group of 20 travel managers on 'Effective Communication Skills as a Leader.'

At the time I had a four-month-old baby who I was still breast-feeding. It was the middle of summer and on that day I chose to wear a light blue cotton shirt. Halfway through the presentation I could feel my left breast leaking — I'd forgotten to wear breast pads.

Halfway through the presentation I could feel my left breast leaking — I'd forgotten to wear breast pads.

My mind went into a spin. I had the horrible thought of 40 eyes watching my shirt get wetter and wetter. Before things became visibly obvious I managed to pick up a glass of water and somehow spill a little on my shirt. Then when the leakage showed, people would think it was from spilling the water rather than what it actually was.

Mireille Ryan

Mireille

Know exactly where you're going

Born and raised in Sydney, Mireille completed science degree at Macquarie University and spent several years rising through the ranks at a major insurance company. After spending three hours commuting each day, she decided to seek a much better work life balance.

Mireille achieved her Cert III in fitness and never looked back. She worked for all the major gyms chains for several years before deciding to open her own fitness business, Health Guru Boot Camp. During this time, she also launched a website, The Busy Mum's Fitness Club, a free membership website where women could access Australia's leading experts on mindset, exercise and nutrition.

Mireille was named 2010 Australian Exercise Professional of the Year by Fitness Australia. Her boot camp business was also a finalist for 2011 Australian Personal Training Business of the Year and won the 2011 QLD Personal Training Business of the Year.

Due to this success, people began seeking her out wanting to know how they could build a successful business. Mireille created her signature brand, "Mireille — Building a Business You Love," which specialises in coaching and mentoring female entrepreneurs and helping them turn their passions into a successful business.

She has appeared on radio, has featured in over 20 magazines around the world, and is a sought after speaker around Australia.

Mireille currently lives on the Gold Coast with her husband Shannon and their three children.

What do you believe it takes to be a professional speaker?

1. **A Desire to Help People.** Successful speakers are passionate about sharing their message and personal experiences with others. I became a public speaker because I wanted to help women build a business that supports them and their families, too. Over the last decade, I have learned so much about what I call "failing forward." These life lessons have really helped me to grow as a business owner and I had a great desire to help others avoid the mistakes I'd made.

2. **Become an expert in your chosen area.** Many people ask me how to become an expert. The first thing I tell them is to learn as much as they can about their topic. I'm a voracious reader — I'll generally spend an hour a day educating myself on my area of expertise. Even if you only spend 20 minutes a day, you'll very quickly know more than the average person about your chosen topic. As my mentor Marty says: "You only need to be an inch above the crowd to be a giant."

3. **Overcome your fear of public speaking.** Over 40% of people fear public speaking — they worry they'll be laughed at or will look stupid. Many doubt they have anything of value to share. It's important to realise you have a message that can help others and by sharing it you can change people's lives. Don't hide your talents! The more you do, the easier it will become.

Do you suffer from nerves and if so, how do you manage them?

Every good speaker suffers from nerves before going on stage. No matter how many talks I do, I still feel a little nervous but it's definitely not like it used to be when I first started out. The best way to overcome your nerves is to just do it. Start with a small group of people and give a five to ten minute talk about something you know well. As you gain more confidence, you can lengthen the time of your talk and speak in front of bigger crowds. Then keep seeking every opportunity you can to speak. The only way you get better at public speaking is by doing it more often and learning from each experience.

Knowing my content settles my nerves. Preparation is key. If I know my talk inside and out then I won't need notes and I'm prepared if someone asks me a question. That takes a lot of the anxiety away.

I always make sure I arrive early enough to familiarise myself with the venue and equipment I'll be using. I then take five minutes in a quiet corner to get myself into the zone — I think about who my audience is and how I can help them. I do some breathing exercises and have a drink of water. Then I'm ready to go.

How do you prepare for a presentation, do you have a specific method you follow and if so what?

When I create one of my signature talks the first thing I do is look at what is causing my potential audience pain. I ask myself: "What keeps my audience awake at night." Do they worry that they don't have enough money and the bills are piling up? I'll take that worry and create a talk that takes them step-by-step how to go from a place of pain to a place of resolution and freedom.

I always use a five-step system to frame my talks. It's less complicated and allows me to walk them through the process. As I go through each step, I generally go "deep dish" on one step to give them a lot of content. That way, by the end of my talk, I've given every person there something solid they can take away. This also allows me to sell my products, which go through each of the steps in more detail.

How do you customise your presentation to meet the needs of the audience?

I heard it said once that you don't change your talk — you change your audience. With that in mind, I create talks that have excellent content regardless of the industry I'm speaking to. I also customise it using examples from the industry I'm speaking to. For your talk to be effective you'll need to show your audience how they can take the information from your talk and implement it themselves.

 Don't change your talk — change your audience.

What business are you in and what services does it offer?

I'm CEO of Health Guru Industries, a business that helps women build mind, body and business via three business brands:

- **FitMind** helps women build a strong mindset or, as we say, building muscle for your mind

- **Health Guru Boot Camp** helps women build healthy bodies for life

- **Mireille — Building a Business You Love.** I coach and mentor female business owners and entrepreneurs, working with them to build a strong business brand, attract more ideal clients and build a profitable business.

What do you believe was your biggest sacrifice in getting the business off the ground?

Time, because I had to do everything myself. I was the person who ran the client sessions, did the accounts, did the customer service, did the marketing and social media and built the business. You wear many hats when you start a small business. As my business grew, I began delegating these tasks to my team.

Money, because everything I earned I pumped back into the business. I didn't draw a wage for a very long time. I was blessed that my husband had full time work.

These sacrifices weren't hard for me to make because I always knew where I was going. From the very first day I knew my company would go national. How? I just knew it deep inside. I had a very strong desire to help people all over the country so I didn't limit myself to a local area. Seven years down the track, I've launched nationally with massive growth planned across the country and beyond in the near future.

What have you found are the best methods or strategies for keeping motivated and focussed?

It's important to love what you do. I'm so passionate about my business that it doesn't feel like work. I could get up early and work all day long and way into the night and not even feel like I'm working. This passion drives me forward so it isn't even a conscious decision to stay motivated. This is important in the early days when money isn't quite flowing. If it doesn't feel like work you'll do it regardless.

Passion is also important when you have major setbacks, too. I remember one of my past employees leaving and stealing 15 of my clients at a cost to me of $20,000. I had mentored them and felt extremely let down and upset. My passion got me through the hard times. Instead of giving up, I was determined to push on and build a business that attracted the right type of people.

The other important way to stay motivated and focussed is to have a plan. I didn't work from a plan at the start. I just did what needed to be done. I found I was constantly busy and didn't seem to be getting anywhere. I also suffered from a common disease entrepreneurs call "Bright Shiny Object" syndrome. This is where any good idea distracts you from your path and takes you off on a tangent. I found I had lots of projects on the go but none completed and they were sucking my time and resources.

Now I have a 50-page business plan I work to, so I know exactly where I am going. I know what tasks I need to achieve and what tasks I need to delegate. I also see a mentor each week that asks me these important questions:

1. How many phone calls have I made this week?

2. How many appointments have I completed this week?

3. How much money have I personally brought in to the business?

He keeps me focussed on the goals and tasks that build my business and not get distracted by things that don't help me achieve these three things. He's also shown me my business' potential.

When I studied successful business people, they all had mentors or participated in masterminds. I'm a huge believer that every business owner should have a business mentor. It's the fast track to success.

Who are the mentors that have inspired you? What important lessons have you learnt from them?

I follow and learn from a lot of people. I'm a big fan of Napoleon Hill's *"Think and Grow Rich"* — I think every businessperson should be read it. I also love Jim Rohm, Jack Canfield, Bob Proctor and Robert Kiyosaki.

My first mentors were in the US fitness industry. I paid to be coached by them for 12 months. I also travelled to Los Angeles and met with a fitness industry leader, spending three hours being personally coached in his home.

My mentors have taught me these two important lessons:

1. **Know exactly where you are going** — start with the end in mind. Decide where you want to be in five years and reverse engineer your business so you know exactly how to get there and what resources you need in place to achieve your goals.

2. **The importance of systems** — Business systems let you can create brand consistency that allows others to work with you and grow your business. Systems save you time and money — the two things most entrepreneurs struggle with. Over the last couple of years, I have managed to take myself totally out of servicing clients in my fitness business. Rather I focus on growing the business.

Do you have a mentor today? If so, who is it and why?

My mentor is Marty Morris. Marty has been able to help build businesses from inception to $100 million in two to three years. He is CEO of MMI International and is a recognised authority on peak performance and performance management.

He has shown me that it takes as much work to create a $10 million business as it does a $1 million business, so why not create a $10 million business. He's helped me turn my small business brands into a corporation prepared for fast growth over the next three years. He's helped me with my business structure, to create a business plan, given me direction and advice and, most importantly, holds me accountable to KPIs in my role as CEO. I know I wouldn't be able to do what I do now without his advice and guidance.

Do you practice your personal development even now?

I practice personal development on a daily basis. I read personal development books. I listen to business and marketing podcasts as I drive between appointments. I'm a firm believer of the University of the car! In fact, I reward my team for doing the same. Each one of my team reads a minimum of 18 minutes a day. In a few short months I've seen their personal growth.

Recently I was listening to a video clip from Jim Rohn. He said something very profound that has stuck with me: "Learn to work harder on yourself than you do your job… If you work hard on your job, you make a living. If you work hard on yourself, you can make a fortune."

My personal development time is so important — I wake up early to make sure I get it in before I start the day. I know by growing myself I'll grow my opportunities and my success.

 Decide where you want to be in five years. People spend more time planning a holiday than their life.

Is there a significant quote or saying that you live by?

"What ever the mind can conceive, it can achieve." — Napoleon Hill

If I can see it in my mind first, then I know I can do it.

Another of my favorites is: "Success leaves clues" — so learn what successful people do and follow their example.

What is the first step that someone could take if they decided to follow in your footsteps today?

Decide where you want to be in five years. People spend more time planning a holiday than their life. Know exactly where you are going and enlist the help of others to help you get there. I have a list of 100 things of I want to do in my life.

One of those goals was to become QLD Exercise Professional of the Year. When I wrote that goal down, I was a stay-at-home mum who had a small business with two young kids at school and a toddler who sat on my lap as I worked.

Within two years I achieved this goal *and* was named Australian Exercise Professional of the Year Did it require I put in a lot of effort — yes. But if I hadn't written that goal down I know I wouldn't have achieved it.

Another tip is to spend time with people who've already achieved what you want to achieve. If you want to be a successful speaker, spend time with people who are already successful speakers. If you want a million dollar business, spend time with people who have already built million dollar businesses. I'm a big believer that you become like the people you most closely associate with. Being around successful people rubs off.

Narelle Lee

Narelle Lee

Challenge Boundaries and Push the Envelope

Narelle Lee is a performance strategist and behavioural specialist who uses the latest research and frameworks in neuroscience and positive psychology to assist her clients realise their fullest potential and achieve the business and personal outcomes they desire.

She believes that passionate, high-performing people deliver profits, helping her clients to create engaged, dynamic workplaces and high performing teams that contribute to the bottom line.

Using her extensive senior corporate experience and learnings from some of life's larger curve balls, Narelle inspires and engages audiences of all ages and backgrounds.

She is an author of numerous magazine articles, audio recordings and is a contributor to several books with new titles in the works. Her formal business qualifications include an MBA and she blends this with Master Practitioner of NLP, Time Line therapy (TM) and Hypnosis.

When she is not writing, speaking or working with executives and teams, Narelle is a proud back-of-the-pack age group Ironman triathlete and lives in Sydney with her husband and a very large, hairy Alaskan malamute.

Do you suffer from nerves and how do you manage them?

I'd be lying if I said no. My view is all good presenters suffer from nerves to some extent, but the distinction between good speakers and also-rans is how they harness the nerves.

I find that tension before a presentation is what moves me forward — actors talk about this as well.

My nerve management strategies are simple:

- **Be prepared** — rehearse the presentation or speech in the mirror and even better video it and review it

- **Know your content** — unless the presentation is some form of adlib contest, know the material — this ensures that I am able to answer questions that may arise, and not look silly

- **Use positive anchors before taking the stage** — I fire off anchors that take me to a headspace of total confidence

- **Stop and breathe**

- **Stand tall, head up and smile**

What sort of training and development did you undertake?

My training began when I was four years old. My father's secretary had just qualified as a Speech and Drama teacher, so I got sent to "elocution" lessons, which I pursued until my senior year at high school. Standing on stage, stagecraft and being in front of audiences became an integral part of me. Being on stage was a way of meeting one of my core needs — significance — so it was never really a challenge.

At school I won various speaking and presentation. During my corporate career I regularly presented to audiences of all types, including non-English speaking audiences where I needed to speak through an interpreter. I attended several presentation skills courses to improve my craft as part of my career development.

I now take every opportunity to observe outstanding speakers and learn even more about how to deliver an engaging presentation.

How Did You Build Your Confidence as a Speaker?

I built my confidence through practicing my craft and using the technical knowledge learned in presentation skills courses, my Speech and Drama training as well as finding "safe" audiences to speak to.

In my experience, most audiences don't want a speaker to fail. Knowing this has helped build confidence along the way. I also master my subject matter — being able to walk onto the platform as an expert in a subject is a significant contributor to greater confidence.

Knowing I have rehearsed my presentation over and over out loud also gives me confidence I know the content, that my presentation will run to time and is engagingly written for all behavioural types. I also practice using props and audio-visual equipment to make sure I'm not "fluffing" around with slides or can't use controls.

Practice using props and audiovisual equipment to make sure I'm not "fluffing" around with slides or can't use controls.

How do you customise your presentation to meet the needs of the audience?

The first thing I do is obtain a brief from the client to establish the background of the audience — who is likely to be in the room and what is the client's objective for the event? Then I can begin to tailor my presentations to suit the audience demographic and psychographic profile.

For example, when speaking to a largely non-English speaking audience, I would make adjustments to language, phrases and anecdotes and the analogies I use. If there's one particular ethnic group, I'll incorporate cultural elements as far as possible. If I'm speaking to a group of senior business executives the language, pace and tempo of my presentation is quite different. Similarly, how I physically present myself also changes — I would tend to be less formal in an inner city community instance than with senior business executives.

In short, I endeavor to be on the same page as my audience as far as possible.

I also make sure my presentation covers off all four behavioural styles. I include something for everyone — paying particular attention to engaging those who are likely to have the shortest attention span first.

 I endeavor as far as possible to be on the same page as my audience.

What techniques do you use to achieve your goals?

I've been a goal setter since my early teenage years. But I use a more structured framework now — I used to just make a list on a piece of paper.

I once found a list several years after I had written it, filed and forgotten. I was amazed to discover I could actually tick it off — even though at the time I wrote the list I had no idea how to achieve my goals. If I ever entertained any doubt about the power of goal setting, this completely wiped it out.

My process is simple — I start with the end in mind (my 'Big Why' — why do I want to do this or have this?) I then answer three key questions for each of the key areas of my life:

- Who do I have to be to do this/have this?

- What do I need to start, maintain and finish so that I do/have this?

- What am prepared to do or not prepared to do to have this?

I then set yearly, three yearly and long term goals each question, which I'll go on to break down into 90-day, 30-day, weekly and daily goals. This makes my goals easier to track, easier to adjust if I start to head off target, and allows me to chunk goals into manageable pieces.

It also allows me to adjust to any new opportunities that present themselves — so at any one time I have a goal that's reachable. Small chunks give the opportunity to build in small celebrations along the way and also reduce any chance of becoming overwhelmed due to the enormity of the total goal.

I'm highly visual, so I create a vision board containing images symbolising my goals and make sure it's somewhere I can see it every day. This means I'm engaging my reticular activation system and setting my unconscious mind to work. I keep a screensaver with a picture that represents something I'm working towards and a photo of my dream car on my phone.

Another strategy I've found particularly useful, taken from Napoleon Hill's *Think & Grow Rich*. I remove wriggle room — where I can, I'll put myself in a position to "put it out there" to an audience that I'm intending something. This is my interpretation of the "don't leave options open" that Napoleon Hill talks about.

What have you found are best methods or strategies for keeping motivated and focussed

To some extent it depends on the particular outcome or life area I am working on.

I have a natural tendency to be internally motivated, so I play mind games with myself and create little challenges. For example, when I am running a marathon or doing long swim training sets and I begin to find myself thinking that I might like to stop, I focus on the person in front of me and pretend there's a big piece of fishing line attached to them and I am holding the fishing rod, and I mentally see myself winding the reel and reeling them in — this keeps me moving forward towards my goal.

Taking this thinking into other areas of my life, I find that breaking my goals into small chunks that I can tick off and can celebrate their completion, keeps me motivated.

I use anchoring a lot. I put myself into the state I want to experience such as highly motivated and focussed and I anchor that. This allows me to return to that state any time I choose, and I find this especially useful when there are tasks that I must do that I know I need to do, but which are not my favourite things to be doing. Anchoring is one of the keys I use to ensure I walk onto the stage totally confident.

Another way I stay motivated is to hang with like minded people — people who are committed to excellence and achieving their dreams. Probably one of the most motivating places I can think of is the race village at a major marathon or Ironman — and then to be on the finish line as finishers complete their event, it absolutely fires me up.

My other favourite is the feeling of walking onto stage, the spotlights with the blur of faces in the audience, and giving an award winning presentation — I often take myself back to that feeling when I walk into a room for the first time.

Do you continue to practice your personal development even now?

Most certainly, I do! I'm a lifelong learner and I'll never stop looking for new ways to be the best version of me I can be. I believe I'll always strive for more and challenge myself.

The form that this takes may vary from time to time. I'm open to any opportunity for personal growth. I'm a reader of books on topics that help me grow and am always on the lookout for new thinking in the area of personal development so I can integrate it into the work I do with my clients and also my own life.

Is there a significant quote or saying that you live by?

> "I'm always on the lookout for new thinking." — Henry Drummond.

I've lived by this credo. I often bite off more than I can chew and I'm grateful my husband gives me the space to explore what I can possibly do.

In most cases I find I'm able to come through — my most significant periods of personal growth have occurred when I've undertaken things using this perspective. Incredible experiences spring from challenging boundaries and pushing the envelope.

Incredible experiences spring from challenging boundaries and pushing the envelope.

When I stop listening to those who tell me I can't do it, focus my mind on the strength and inner determination and really switch it "on," any overwhelming situation fades away. Perhaps I have an inflated opinion of what I can do — but I firmly believe when I truly believe something is possible, I can do it. It may not happen at the first attempt or the way I originally expected, but it does happen.

Did you ever want to give up because it all got too much?

Yes, there have been instances where I've felt I was in too deep. Throwing my hands in the air seemed like the easiest option but I can genuinely say I didn't, I pushed through. I don't admit defeat easily. This stubborn streak has always served me well over the years.

Persistence is one of my highest values. I keep going. I may not always end up where I wanted or followed the path I originally thought. Sometimes the work around has created a far better outcome than my original path. There's always more than one way to skin a cat and challenges that pop up remind me to test my ability to think laterally.

I draw on my sport analogies in other parts of my life. There have been times during marathons or Ironman that I've stopped and recorded a Did Not Finish, but this was only after a deep soul search to work out whether or not my wanting to stop was driven by mind over matter or because I was genuinely at risk of injury. Knowing the difference is key to success. Sometimes it becomes obvious that I'm on the wrong path but rather than give up I'll regroup and look for a path that will move me forward.

> *Sometimes it becomes obvious that I'm on the wrong path but rather than give up I'll regroup and look for a path that will move me forward.*

Apart from material possessions, money brings opportunity. Can you share opportunity you are most proud of that money has given you?

This is a hard question — the more I think about it, there are quite a few in different parts of my life. There are two top of mind — both centred on my lifelong passions.

Both experiences occurred around Chengdu in China. My husband and I are passionate about animal welfare and this is very much part of my Big Why.

After much planning and organising, we were permitted to spend a day at the Animal Asia Moon Bear Rescue Centre outside Chengdu. It was a roller coaster of emotions as we started the day being shown with no detail spared the horrific treatment the magnificent bears endure during their time in the bile farms. This was one of the most harrowing experiences of my life and it touched me deeply.

We moved from this horror to the jubilation of seeing the rescued bears enjoying freedom in their wonderful enclosures full of ponds, climbing sets, treats and of course grass under their feet. This was an opportunity very few westerners get to experience and I'm grateful we've had the means and persistence to make this journey.

The other occurred during the same trip to China deep in the mountains (and the clouds) to the south of Chengdu to Wolong — a panda research and breeding centre where around 80% of the world's captive pandas are located. Getting there was probably the most hair-raising road trip we have ever undertaken — up 3000 metres in the dark, no guardrails between us and the gorges thousands of metres below.

During our two-day stay, we experienced pandas in a way very few will. We were in an enclosure with about eight juvenile pandas and we were literally sitting in the mud having them crawl all over us, try to steal our backpacks and demand to be patted. We were there for a very long time

We also watched as Chinese carers tenderly attended to the cubs in humidicribs. We witnessed the excitement of the Chinese media and staff as twins were born. We are very grateful for this trip — a few months afterwards the area was destroyed by a massive earthquake. The pandas have only recently returned.

What do you think stops people from achieving the level of success they desire?

First, they're not truly clear about why they want it, what it means and, by extension, who they need to be to get there.

Successful people persist — they don't give up when things get a bit tough. They embrace failures as learning experiences. Unsuccessful people walk away and tend to lay blame externally. They lack ownership of their outcomes and tend to live in a world of "because."

The unsuccessful tend not to want to move beyond their comfort zone. They'll look for quick fixes whereas successful people are prepared to do what it takes.

I believe success is a function of mindset and action. Successful people often have an 'abundance mindset' while the unsuccessful through a lens of lack and scarcity.

Finally (this is probably an extension of the comfort zone point), unsuccessful people are limited by fear — of being cut off from their "tribe" or not being good enough. They haven't engaged their personal power.

Successful people persist — they don't give up when things get a bit tough.

What is the most you have spent in a single transaction?

About $105K purchasing my first SLK Mercedes Benz back around 1996. Why I bought it is a little hard to explain, but in some ways it sums up how I live my life.

The car was bright yellow and on a turntable at the Motorshow — it was before they were even available in Australia, so Benz was in a sort of pre-launch mode. I walked in, decided then and there I wanted it and moreover, was going to have it. Why I wanted it was probably a function of my passion for uniqueness — at the time the car was certainly "out there" and part of me has always embraced standing out and being unique.

At that time I had a highly paid job in a prestigious company but I still could not put hand on heart and say I could afford the car. But delivery was two and half years away, so my logic was I could take advantage of the great leasing packages available at the time and lease another Mercedes to drive in the meantime. I'd trust I would have the money to pay for it when it finally landed in Australia. In other words I backed myself in.

And it worked. By the time the dealer called to say the car had arrived I had the money to pay for it. I was able to achieve my goal down by focussing my unconscious mind on the outcome and the decisions I made as a result. I was definitely looking at life through a lens of abundance. It was also the manifestation of a long term goal I had set myself and maintained from my early teenage years — that I would drive a Mercedes convertible — reinforcing my firm belief in the power of goal setting and visualisations.

What keeps you from lying on the beach all day?

I'm driven to achieve some fairly big contribution goals and, at this point in my life, I haven't reached a level of financial independence where I could begin to fulfil them but it goes beyond that.

I don't see myself ever retiring — I see myself working in some capacity for a long time. I'm aiming at having the flexibility to choose when I work and with whom I work, but not stopping totally. I need the mental stimulation, the social interaction (work meets some of my need for connection) and the challenge that working brings and if I'm working at my passion, then it isn't work.

I don't ever want to get to the point in my life where the highlight of my day is going to bingo or Aldi.

And I get really sunburnt, so I can't sit on the beach all day!

Pat Rae

Take Massive Action Now

Pat began his working life as a police officer in 1985, as a "wet behind the ears" 19-year-old in South Auckland, New Zealand. Shortly after he was diagnosed with hypertension, something doctors put down to his career. By age 30 he was on blood pressure medication and told to lose weight, a bizarre request for a 6 foot 2 inches tall, 110 kg Police officer and representative rugby player at his peak.

In 1997, Pat resigned from the Police and shifted to sunnier skies where he entered the seedy world of private investigations in Australia. Nicknamed "N.G.U" by his peers for "never giving up" he was involved in a number of high profile investigations including the civil case surrounding the death of former Australian cricketer, David Hookes.

At the same time, Pat was forging a very successful sporting career as a rugby union referee travelling to some of the world's top sporting arenas as a match official. However, his constant weight battle and ailing health prompted him to make some dramatic life style changes and in 2006 he became a personal trainer and stumbled onto the secret that enabled him to win his weight loss battle and improve his health. He no longer has to be medicated nor does he have high blood pressure, a feat his cardiologist said would never happen.

Pat soon became sought after as a motivational speaker because of his humour and expertise in changing people's lives and holding an audience.

His business, Pat Rae Personal Training and massage therapy clinic in Springwood, Brisbane employs a great team of trainers, remedial massage therapists and lifestyle coaches all working together to tackle Australia's obesity epidemic head on. He also has an online membership program that enables him to provide exercise programmes, meal plans, stretching programs and motivational videos all over the world.

An internationally published author and regular contributor to the South City Bulletin, Pat is married with three children and a grandfather. In his spare time Pat sings, plays the guitar, trains dogs to be obedient and in 1991 was voted the second best father of the year.

What do you believe it takes to be a professional speaker?

To become a professional speaker you need three prerequisites:

1. A clear and compelling message to a very specific audience

2. An even more compelling reason for spreading that message

3. A dogged determination to keep delivering that message even when there appears to be no-one listening.

This may sound a little bit dribbly but it's absolutely true. In my own case, my message is directed at a very small niche market and is simple — people over 35 can slow the aging process and live a longer, healthier and wealthier life by simply eating real wholefoods (preferably organic), adding lifting weights to their exercise regime, stretch every second day to combat twenty-first century sedentary lifestyle habits and love your family.

I've watched a ton of family members die years before their life expectancy age because they have ignored all the warning signs. They've smoked too much, drank way too much alcohol, eaten a poorly designed nutritional program all their adult life (too many carbohydrates and not enough quality protein) and have done little or no exercise.

How do you prepare for a presentation, do you have a specific method you follow and if so what is it?

To write and develop a talk, whether it's ten minutes or three days, I follow an exacting formula that was taught to me by my mentor. It worked for him and it works for me, so why bother changing a successful plan, right? So here's my magic formula:

INTRODUCTION

The best way to get yourself pumped up before you even hit the podium is to make sure that you have an awesome and inspirational biography ready to go and read to the awaiting audience by the person hosting the event. It's vitally important that by the time you hit the stage you don't have to talk about yourself, so I always get someone else to introduce me. The last thing an audience wants to happen when they attend is to have someone they've never met rant on about how wonderful and fantastic they are, so DON'T. The key, get someone else to do it for you.

WIIFM

Making a great first impression is vital, not only in every day meet and greets but also when you walk out on stage. So to ensure that I make a great first impression I like to use the introduction as a way to get the audience on side and the best way to do this is to make the talk ALL ABOUT THEM. Your introduction told them who you are, what you do, how long you've been doing it and what your talk is all about, so in the first 30 seconds as a professional speaker you must ask them exactly what it is they want from the talk. I do this by asking them at least three simple questions. That way you can identify what burning problem they possess that your talk could potentially solve for them

BIHAG

Once I know what the audience wants, I promise to deliver to them some information that can help them solve their problem or issue. I tell the audience that I'll be asking them at the end of the talk if I delivered on my promise and that I'll be making an offer to them at the end of my talk

PROOF

I then provide them with some evidence that what I'm about to share with them actually works and this is usually in the form of some social proof like testimonials from people whom I've previously worked with and have achieved some form of benefit from working with me.

CONTENT

When it comes to the content, I make a point of choosing only two of key strategies to focus on. Anymore and the audience tend to suffer from information overload and the best way to highlight those key strategies is to tell real life stories. For example in one of my more popular talks on back pain I demonstrate the art of belly breathing by showing a short video of my then three-year-old daughter fast asleep on a bean bag in front of the TV. It clearly shows the act of belly breathing and it's personal.

CALL TO ACTION

Once I've finished with the actual content of my talk, I confirm with them that what I've told them was what I promised to deliver at the start and then I make some sort of offer or call to action. It can vary between gifts in exchange for their details or maybe I might make an actual sales offer, like a book, a DVD, or even a ticket to an event. It really all depends on who the audience is and how long I'm permitted to speak to them for.

What kind of training/development did you undertake to become the speaker you are today?

I've always been a confident person, a trait my parents instilled in me from an early age. We were never well off but we always had food on the table and a roof over our heads. My mum was the musician in the house. She could sing and play the guitar so performing was a natural extension of that and that was when I first got up on stage.

At high school, we never had a debating team but we had 15 rugby teams every Saturday morning. So a bunch of us convinced our English teacher we ought to submit a debating team in the local high school debating competition. It was a great way to meet girls and though we didn't win many debates it was my first experience in talking on stage (as opposed to singing).

A few years later I had the dubious task of being MC at a close friends wedding. The feedback I got inspired me to take a closer look at speaking for a living. However, it wasn't till I became a personal trainer that the opportunity to really stretch my speaking legs took off. I started running workshops and seminars as a method of driving more clients into my fitness business. I identified early on it was easier to perform a sales presentation to a room full of people than to one person.

I met one of my mentors Paul Blackburn via a chance email that hit my junk box one day — he really transformed by professional speaking. He formalised my entire speaking methodology and opened a few mindset doors I never knew existed. After attending one of Paul's three-day workshops I invested in a 12-month coaching program on how to become a professional public speaker. And the rest is history.

Do you have a product, program or other offering that you present for sale at speaking events? Do you recommend this for new speakers?

The short answer is yes, however it's not quite that simple. When I speak I always have a call to action at the end. The only difference is what do I want my audience to do once I've finished speaking? The answer to this question is always governed by the speaking environment and length of time I'm permitted to speak.

For instance, I'm often asked to speak at breakfast business networking meetings and, while the length of time I get to talk varies, it usually falls somewhere between the 10-30 minute length. At talks of this nature, you don't really get an opportunity to sell anything because the length of time you're in front of your audience doesn't really give you the chance to build up sufficient rapport and credibility to have them saying, "Yes please! Where can I buy what you're offering?"

So I usually give a small gift away for free in exchange for their name, mobile and email address. The gift will also vary, depending on the audience's age and gender. For example:

- For an all-female small business owners' presentation, I gave a 20-minute talk entitled: "It's OK to Look Fat When You Breathe," designed to teach you how to breathe using your diaphragm, thereby activating a major postural muscle and hopefully reducing any lower back pain you might be suffering. I show a short video of my 3-year-old daughter asleep on a beanbag to demonstrate my point and make the talk. At the end I offer my free e-book, "10 Step Plan to Healthy Living" in exchange for their personal details.

- At a predominantly male, middle/upper management business breakfast I may talk about, "The Saber-Toothed Tiger is Still Making You Fat." This quickly demonstrates how stress is a leading cause of belly fat in middle-aged men. At the end, I have another free e-book available, "My 15 Top Tips to Fat Loss."

- If I'm talking to potential clients for my personal training studio, such as a group involved in a local weight loss challenge, then I'll need about 30-45 minutes of speaking time to offer them one of my Kick Start Packs (3 x 60-minute personal training sessions).

As a general rule, the longer you're speaking to an audience the more rapport and credibility you build up with them, and the more chances you've got of getting them to say 'yes' to those four burning questions they'll have going off in their head. Questions like: "Do I like you? Do

I trust you? Do I need what you've got, and do I want it NOW?" And when they say 'yes' to all four right there and then, you'll gain a new customer.

 As a general rule, the longer you're speaking to an audience the more rapport and credibility you build up with them, and the more chances you've got of getting them to say 'yes' to those four burning questions they'll have going off in their head.

Did you always know the career path you wanted to take? If not, where did you start from and how did you make the change?

I've really only had two careers in my life: law enforcement and health/fitness. I fell into both by accident.

In 1984, during my last year of high school, I was lucky enough to be selected for the New Zealand Secondary Schools Rugby team to tour the UK, Ireland and Holland. Some famous All Blacks emerged from that team along with a famous rugby world cup winning coach. The tour went for 2 months and included playing test matches on some of the rugby world's most hallowed grounds.

Unfortunately, when I returned home I found myself out of school, unemployed, with no aspirations of attending university and all alone. Then the New Zealand Police lowered the retiring age for its staff from 65 to 55 and the mass exodus of Police officers created a sudden shortage. The four-month course seemed a breeze compared to the five years I'd just completed at boarding school. So I joined up and for the next 15 years policed the streets of South Auckland, rural South Waikato and the gorgeous Hawkes Bay.

However, a marriage breakup found me seeking home comforts so I packed my bags and moved to the sunny skies of Brisbane in Australia. While attending a rugby game shortly after, I met a Wallaby by the name of Dan Crowley at the bar. We got chatting. He had recently left the Queensland Police Service and had set his own private investigations company.

Next thing you know I'm a private investigator. I got to work on some very interesting cases. At the same time, I was forging a very successful sporting career as a rugby union referee and it was during this period of my life that my passion for health and fitness was ignited. Fast-forward another 10 years and here I am today, a personal trainer, massage therapist, holistic lifestyle coach and motivational speaker. The bulk of my public speaking talks and presentations are based around my take on health and fitness.

What business are you in and what services does it offer?

I'm involved in a couple of business interests. I own a small personal training studio. Our target market is people who feel uncomfortable in the gym environment. We focus predominantly on simply getting people moving again so that they can slow or even stop the aging process, lose some body fat and regain some flexibility throughout their joints.

It still amazes me today how poorly most people living in the twenty-first century move. Included in the service provided is remedial massage and holistic lifestyle support. I've developed an online personal training system for those unable to come see me personally. Various workouts, meal plans, stretching programs and assessment tools are accessed through my online membership portal.

My public speaking business is based around my health and fitness message. I speak to schools, business networking events, clubs, community organisations and small/medium businesses. I talk on a range of topics that benefit the average everyday person to become a better, stronger, fitter and healthier person.

I also partner with another Melbourne fitness trainer to offer a business-mentoring program for other fitness professionals ranging from free resources, two-day business boot camps and 12-module coaching programs.

What techniques do you use to achieve your goals?

Goal setting can be quite a controversial subject to cover because there are so many different methods. I've tried a number of them, all with varying levels of success and failure. The technique I use today is a combination of two or three popular ones. It goes something like this:

1. **Get yourself a goal book.** Record your goals in a formalised bounded book of some description. The more you spend on purchasing the book the better. Mine is a leather bound one my partner gave me as a gift. She's personally inscribed on the inside cover and it holds a very special place in my heart. I carry it everywhere I go and I read it twice a day.

2. **Follow the SMARTIE formula for writing goals**

    The SMART acronym, in my opinion, doesn't quite go far enough and that was where I failed with goal setting. I've taken the acronym a couple of stages further to SMARTIE. Still be specific, measurable, achievable, realistic and timeframe bound, but add Inspirational and Emotional for some extra clout. Oh, and make sure to date and time your goal entry.

3. **Write your goals in present tense**

    I used to make the mistake of writing a goal as something that I wanted to achieve AT SOME FUTURE POINT IN TIME. For example, I once wrote a goal, "To referee at the 2007 Rugby World Cup." At the time I had just been selected to the Australian Rugby Union's Referee Program and it wasn't such a pipe dream.

The problem with writing a goal in future speak is that it never comes, because no matter what you do to achieve it, whenever you go over your goal or re-read it, it's always written as if it has never been reached. Oh, I never did achieve that goal by the way.

So instead of writing goals in future speak, write them in present tense. Write them as though you are in the midst of actually experiencing them. Make sure you use emotional and inspirational feelings as if you can reach out and touch them. This is crucial, because having that inspirational and emotional attachment is the "WHY" and, as Robert Kyosaki writes in *Rich Dad Poor Dad*, the "WHY must be bigger than the "WHAT."

4. **Read your goal book twice a day — last thing at night and first thing in the morning OUT LOUD!!**

    This step is crucial in maintaining focus. Have you ever embarked on a plan of some description, only to have your confidence shattered by close family and friends? Why is it that we often listen to the opinion of our close family and friends who have no expertise or interest in OUR goals?

    The ONLY person you really need to listen to and believe is yourself. So this is why it is critical to read your goals OUT LOUD to yourself, twice a day — last thing at night and first thing in the morning. The more you hear something, the more you tend to believe it and the more likely it is to come true.

    You also move your goals from the conscious to the subconscious mind, which is where you want them to be. Once firmly planted in your subconscious, your goals will be easily recalled — whenever you lose focus, you'll know where to come back to. With focus, whenever we get hit with the "Self Doubt Punch" we can come back to where we feel comfortable.

5. **Include how achieving your goal makes you feel "in your goal"**

   The WHY in anything is much bigger than the WHAT? People I work with often want to lose weight but when I ask them why they often have no reply.

   This is the main reason why so many people fail to achieve their weight loss goals. They have no idea why they are doing it and so when the going gets rough (as it always does in anything), they have no driving force behind them. So, when writing down your goal, make sure you include how you will feel to have achieved it. Be as specific as you want — there's no point in holding back here.

6. **Stick in cultured pictures that help emotionalise your goals**

   For those of you more visually orientated, you may want to stick cultured pictures in your goal book to help you visualise them. This will assist you to build a physical picture of what your goal will feel like when you achieve it.

7. **Make audio recordings of your goals**

   For those of you who are auditory focussed (only 7% of the population and I'm one of them), make recordings of you reading your goals OUT LOUD. Or, instead of reading them, listen to them. There's a simple free software program called Audacity (http://audacity.sourceforge.net) that lets you make audio recordings on your computer with just a microphone. You can edit recordings (remove all your ums and ahs), then convert them into MP3 files, save them to a playlist and listen in on your IPod.

8. **Have definitive plans to achieve your goals**

   Like anything, if you fail to plan, you plan to fail. Writing down a plan to achieve anything in life is crucial.

I once built a deck. That may not sound like much to you, but before I built it, I attended deck-building classes at Bunnings, took a TAFE technical drawing course and then drew scaled plans using a free CAD software program. Once I'd drawn the deck (it took me four attempts to get it right), I took the plans back to Bunnings and sourced all my materials. I then took a week off work, worked like a tradie from 7.00am — 4.30pm building this deck (and I drank a six-pack every day after work).

9. **Take MASSIVE ACTION immediately**

Don't wait until your plans are fully completed before taking massive action. DO IT NOW!!! This is where all great plans fall down. People don't actually take any action. I used to work with a salesperson who I would say was ALL talk. You know the kind of person I'm referring to. They say lots but do nothing. Don't let that be you. Take massive action. Your plans can change over time to reflect changes and that's OK, but don't wait for the perfect plan before starting otherwise, guess what… you'll never ACTUALLY start

10. **Review your goals on a regular basis**

Regardless of whether you achieve them or not, make sure you periodically review your goals. Financial goals can be reviewed at the end of the financial year, with monthly or three-monthly check-ups to track your progress. Annual goals can be reviewed at Christmas, which is a great time for reflection. Spiritual goals can be reviewed at religious occasions. Health and fitness goals can be reviewed at various sporting accomplishments. Whatever your goal is, ensure you've factored in regular reviews to track your progress.

> *The ONLY person you really need to listen to and believe is yourself. So this is why it is critical to read your goals OUT LOUD to yourself, twice a day — last thing at night and first thing in the morning. The more you hear something, the more you tend to believe it and the more likely it is to come true.*

What have you found are the best methods or strategies for keeping motivated and focussed?

By simply reading your goal book twice a day or listening to your own goals via an mp3 file, you avoid the chances of becoming demotivated because you're goals are "in your face." Staying focussed becomes irrelevant because your vision is crystal clear. After a period of reading your goals to yourself out loud, they'll be committed to your subconscious memory and become truths, NOT goals.

Here's an example: Ask yourself, how old are you and how do you know? The common response is "I have a driver's license, passport or birth certificate with a date of birth on it." But, in reality, the only people who can really testify as to your rightful age are those who were present at your birth. You can't really say when you were born because you simply don't know. You simply believe your birthday falls on a particular date, because you've been repeatedly told that through birthday celebrations every year on the same day.

At some stage in your life, your birthday transcended from being just another day in the calendar to the day you honestly believe you were born on. How did this happen? How did this day become your birthday? Through constant, out loud repetition — and that's exactly how goals become truths. You say your goal out loud long and often enough and, trust me, no one on this earth will be able to convince you that your goal is some pie-in-the-sky waffled out dream.

Say your goal out loud long and often enough and trust me, no one on this earth will be able to convince you that your goal is some pie-in-the-sky waffled out dream.

Who was your first mentor or inspiration? Do you have mentors today and if so, whom and why?

I've had many mentors in my life. My first were my parents. Mum was a small Maori woman with the strongest and most dogged nature I've ever seen. She was born into borderline poverty with very poor health, which she carried all her adult life. Wrongly diagnosed for many years, it wasn't until my parents migrated to Australia that she discovered she had renal failure. Sadly she passed away at the tender age of 56, finally succumbing to the many health issues that stemmed from two failed kidney transplants and many thousands of related medical procedures.

Dad was your typical, hard-working, blue collar worker who ran away from home at the age of 15 or 16, joined the NZ navy and travelled the world. Both instilled in me that you can do anything you simply set your mind to. Nothing comes easy — you have to work hard for it.

My first paid mentor was Paul Blackburn, the man I credit with teaching me how to become a professional speaker. My mentor today is my business partner Simon Fox. Simon was my teacher when I became a PT. We became friends after I graduated and have kept in touch ever since. I use him to bounce ideas off and to hold me accountable to my action plans. In 2012 we decided to set up a joint venture called Fitness Mentors, providing a mentoring program for other fitness professionals.

Is there a significant quote or saying that you live by?

I don't really live by a favourite quote, although I have a couple that I like to throw around. "Do, or do not, there is no try" (Yoda) and, "Never, ever, ever give up" (anon).

What do you believe are the essential qualities or personal attributes of a successful person?

Success can be measured in a number of different ways and the essential qualities or personal attributes of successful people can also be widely varied. I'm not a great fan of measuring success with cars, houses and bank balances. Too many of my friends with flash cars, big houses and large bank balances also have broken marriages, bitter ex-spouses and kids they never see.

We place too much emphasis on possessions and not enough value on people. If you were to fast-forward to your funeral, do you really think people are going to talk about your BMW X5 or your flash swimming pool? I don't think so. Chances are, they'll remember the wonderful father, loving husband or awesome grandfather that you were.

Successful people share three common traits:

1. They clearly understand that it's NOT ABOUT THE MONEY. Ever wondered why most rich people have charities and give so much away? Because clearly they understand what it's not about.

2. They realise its people that matter, not things. In business, successful people understand that you can't do everything so they learn to delegate. It's better to have someone else do something 80% as good as you can than to have you do everything 100% as good as you.

3. They've learned to use their power for the good of others and not just for personal gain. This, in case you hadn't realised is the true definition of humility.

> *We place too much emphasis on possessions and not enough value on people. If you were to fast-forward to your funeral, do you really think people are going to talk about your BMW X5 or your flash swimming pool? I don't think so.*

What do you think stops people from achieving the level of success they desire?

The one thing that stops people from achieving the level of success they desire is fear — of failure, of what others think. But probably the biggest single thing that holds people back is the fear of being successful.

Let me explain: We go through life these days in a cocoon of protectionism. Parents living in the twenty-first century are often accused of being over protective, of helicopter parenting. You know the ones that hover around their children's every move.

When I grew up, we slept in cots painted with lead paint, drank water out of the garden hose, walked six km to school, played outside till it got dark and then waited till mum screamed out the window that dinner was ready.

Nowadays, kids get driven to and from school and the park, drink bottled water and play on the computer. Is the real world that dangerous that we can't let our kids walk to school? Or is it because we hear horrific news every hour 365 days a year? I suspect the latter.

We're teaching our kids that failure is bad. Some don't even keep score in sporting events. Heaven forbid they should get upset they lost, so let's not bother to score. Failure is NOT bad. Only when we fail do we truly learn. In my PT studio we preach, "FAILURE IS GOOD, QUITTING IS BAD." On occasions I make my clients perform an exercise until they can physically do no more. It's called training to failure. If I see clients simply give up, they get fined. It's all in the mindset.

One of my Dad's favourite sayings was to control the control-ables. In other words, there's no point in worrying about things you've no control over. And one of the things you can never control is what others think. If someone doesn't like you, can you control their thoughts? Of course not, so why bother worrying about it? You may not be able to control other's thoughts, but you certainly can control the way they affect you.

Why do we place so much credence in what others with no expertise think?

Finally, fear of being successful. Most people spend a ton of time placing credibility in the things their family and friends think about areas of expertise they have absolutely no right to provide opinions on.

For example, have you ever gone to a friend's place for a social gathering and mentioned something a little outrageous, like a great new business idea, or some investment scheme? Only to have one of your friends say, "Oh, that won't work, that's a rip off." How do they know? Have they walked in your shoes? Do they possess your drive and dogged determination? Why do we place so much credence in what others with no expertise think? The only person you should be listening to is yourself. And if your own self talk needs a bit of a shake up, get it tuned.

Paul Barrs

Paul Barrs

A true speaker lives what they talk about

Paul is a professional speaker, trainer and business coach teaching all things "internet." Since July 2000 he has helped tens of thousands of small business owners in over 100 countries worldwide grow their online profits and achieve better results through the Internet.

Paul has published over 500 online seminars and regularly speaks for both national and international audiences.

He assists SMEs around the country through direct mentoring and custom coaching, holding monthly workshops on Search Engine Optimisation and Digital Marketing Strategy. He even volunteers time to local programs assisting start-up businesses to assess their digital marketing needs.

What do you believe it takes to be a professional speaker?

Firstly, I'd ask the question, define "professional speaker." Some would say a professional speaker is one who has moved from doing free speaking gigs to paid ones. I would say just because you're being paid doesn't mean you're a professional.

To me, a professional speaker is someone who is trained in the art of public speaking. Yes, it is an art, and yes, training is required for most with exception only to the unique few who are just born with that innate talent. Most of us are not.

What does it take to become a professional speaker? Number one is persistence. It takes courage also to stand in front of others, to say what you have to say and say it with conviction. It's not enough just to convey a message. You must also engage others in that message — if you're in a hostile room this can be more difficult than usual.

So, when starting out I strongly recommend you begin with easy audiences. Test your material lightly. Practice often. And perfect your performance.

What does it take to become a professional speaker? It's the ability to present a message to an audience in an entertaining and engaging way.

How do you prepare for a presentation, do you have a specific method you follow and if so what is it?

Once upon a time, yes, I started out with notes. I started out with bullet points. I would practice by myself in a quiet room for hours to perfect my message. Nowadays if I know my material, it's no problem. I can walk on stage and just speak. Often, if I have PowerPoint slideshows, my bullet points are on the screen before me. If not, I'll use memory strategies, commonly called 'memory pegs', to tag my bullet points in the flow of my message.

Keep in mind this one thing — depending on the audience and how much engagement you have with them, you must also be prepared to take a detour or change direction. Here's the thing. It's far better to speak to an audience than at them. Speak with them, not against them.

 It's far better to speak to an audience than at them.

What are your pre-presentation rituals?

I have only one. Know my material. Not the answer you were looking for, but it's true. If you don't know your material, what's the point? Speaking from a set of notes typed in front of you is not, in my opinion, a quality attributed to a professional speaker. It's the quality of someone who reads well.

To be a professional speaker you must know your material. If you're new in the game then perhaps nerves will still take hold, and I would recommend some kind of quiet breathing exercises. If you're in the motivational game and you think you need to get revved up before you get on stage to get your own levels up then I strongly suggest there's something wrong with your message, because it carries only for a moment.

A true speaker lives what they talk about. They are their message. That doesn't mean you can't speak business in personal circumstances. It simply means you understand it's you speaking, not the topic.

It is good to have pre-presentation rituals, sure. But no amount of 'things to do' can possibly compensate for not knowing your topic.

Speaking from a set of notes typed in front of you is not, in my opinion, a quality attributed to a professional speaker. It's the quality of someone who reads well.

What's your advice for a new and emerging speaker to find guest speaker spots?

Simply this: Have courage and ask. Become part of local networking groups and business events. Look for opportunities where you can volunteer your time in exchange for an opportunity to speak.

Now I'm not talking about pimping your message here. I'm not talking about pimping your product. I'm talking about offering value and high quality, useful, usable information to your audience.

Here's the key. Only speak to people who may be interested in what you have to offer. If they don't have an interest in you or in your topic, you're wasting your time and theirs. It's always about value for them. It's the radio station that all of our customers listen to, WIIFM, 'What's In It For Me?' That's what your audience is asking. You need to make sure you align yourself with such opportunities.

What do you believe was your biggest sacrifice in getting your business off the ground?

This one is easy and difficult for me to answer at the same time. My biggest sacrifice was my family. It was an involuntary sacrifice although I volunteered at the time to give too many hours to my work, too much time to business building things, too much effort to growth and profit and balance sheets, too much self-interest, and not enough self-examination.

My biggest sacrifice? I have a very substantial business now. It gives me everything that I need, and I've now scaled back to find a better balance in life. But, irrespective of what my business could have, should have or did give me, the cost was too high. It cost me my family and, in due course, my health.

I share this with you not with pride but as a stern warning. Please, please, please, please, do not make the same mistake. There's a delusion that many of us fall into as we grow our businesses — 'But if I just get this, if I just do this, if only I can attain, I'll have everything for you.'

Or how about this one? 'Honey, I'm doing this for you and the kids.' One word — bullshit. Say that in front of me and I'll slap you across the face.

The price is too high. It isn't right. Be careful as you plan your progress and look towards your future. The good book says, to what profit is there if a man should gain the world but lose his soul? In much the same way, I say, 'What value is there in having anything when you've lost everything?'

Did you have to change your mindset surrounding public speaking? If so, how did you do it?

This is not the answer commonly given for this question. But I do have a speaking voice. I do have a phone voice. I do have a different mindset when I'm on stage to than when I'm having coffee with friends. Yes, from the moment I walk onto the stage, I'm in performance mode. I'm ready to engage opportunities and entertain. I'm looking for the bright spark in a participant's eye which says, 'I got it.'

This isn't me changing my mindset to become a speaker. I'm fortunate. I've been a speaker my entire life. I was 14 the first time I spoke on stage in the high school play. Yes, I was in a high school musical. And, I had to sing, and it was terrifying. However, over the coming years I continued in theatre and learned the keys to speaking in front of other people.

Have I had to change my mindset regarding my public speaking? No. Now I just live it. It's what I do. It's what I am. I teach, I train, and I help other people whether it's one, 100 or up to 10,000. No matter. To me, being a professional speaker is something that you just do. It's not something you become.

It's either in you waiting to get out or it's a struggle. If it's a struggle, it's not you. You can learn it. You can practice for it. But it's not you. On the other hand, if you've had a burning desire deep inside for as long as you can remember, then yes, being a professional speaker is for you. Go out and do it. Enjoy.

Do you have a mentor today? If so, who is it and why?

My current mentor would be my third in my business career the last 20 odd years and my fourth in life. My business mentor engages me and asks me questions that I'm afraid to ask myself. He checks in on my progress and says, "How're you doing Paul? Have you done what I suggested? Really? Why not?"

He doesn't push me. He knows I can do that myself. But he questions the things that I let go. Sometimes he puts me back on course. Interestingly enough, he never says I should get on stage more or do more of anything.

He is a speaker, coach and trainer himself and, like me, he also runs his own business. He also works in the trenches just like I do each and every day. He speaks from experience. So do I. He leads by example. So do I. He shows kindness and courtesy at all times. I hope so do I.

I follow him and his teaching because I trust him. He is a leader in my eyes because I choose to follow. Simply defined, a leader is one whom others choose to follow. I believe a good professional speaker is also a leader because we must lead by example. My mentor does this. I hope I do this also for others. Food for thought, don't you think?

Is there a significant quote or saying that you live by?

I have many of them. None of them are mine, but over the years I've taken phrases from some of my preferred speakers, memorised them and incorporated them in my own words.

One of the first I ever heard was: "If somebody else can learn to do a thing, then I can learn it too." I don't know who first said it, probably Earl Nightingale, one of the legends, one of the greats. But, this is now one of my core beliefs.

Many years ago, I was very ill, pretty much given up on everything. I wrote out my will — not because I thought I might have to cash it in but as a precaution, while my father reminded me, "There's hope."

All it took for me at that point of time in my life was those two words, "there's hope." That was enough to spark in me and remind me that if somebody else can learn to do a thing, so can I. So, I would say if somebody else can overcome this, so can I. If somebody else can get his or her life back together after this, then so can I.

As I began rebuilding my business, if somebody else who's been through what I've been through can build a successful business then so can I. I then looked more closely at my life and said, 'If someone can build a happy, successful, financially profitable business, and not do it without sacrificing their life, so can I.' So this is my guiding principle, one of many. It's a good one. I suggest you adopt it also.

 "If somebody else can learn to do a thing, then I can learn it, too."

In your opinion, is it harder for women to create significant wealth?

I don't believe so. I hear it all the time about the glass ceiling, about the

Boys' Club, and I do agree to some extent that in the corporate world that this is, I'm sure, true. Do I think it's a good idea? No. Do I believe in equality? No.

I believe that people should be good at what they're good at and get paid well for it. I don't care what sex you are. If you're no good then you shouldn't receive the income for it. But, if you are, then you actually will. You just will.

One of my trainers from years past, Tom Hopkins, said, "We are paid in direct proportion to the value that we offer our customers." If you offer the value that means you'll be paid well for it. More value, more pay.

There are so many opportunities for women these days that we men do not have. But does that mean a woman can't make it, then, in the men's areas? No, of course not. If you're good then you will make it. You simply need to be fired up with persistent and consistent effort. "Never give up, never give up," said Winston Churchill. As long as the price isn't too high then I say to you, never give up. Just keep at it.

Can you describe a typical day in your life? For example, you get up at 5.30am and at the gym by 6am etc.

Okay. Today I got up at 6:00 am. At 7:00 am I hit the gym. I'm home by about 8:30 am. I make up a nice breakfast, following a shower of course. I watch a bit of news while I'm having that.

I check my email. I look at my To Do list and create a bullet point top six for the day. I like a top six, about half a dozen, not too many. Four is okay. Seven or eight is no problem. Twenty? Too much.

I look at my To Do list and create a bullet point top six for the day. I like a top six, about half a dozen, not too many. Four is okay. Seven or eight is no problem. Twenty? Too much.

At the end of the day I will go back to the gym and do some cardio. Weights in the morning, cardio in the afternoon. That's not a typical day. I'm training for something specific at the moment.

During this day I've written an e-newsletter. I've printed out some reports for my SEO customers. I've done some follow ups. I've replied to an event organiser for a workshop I'm giving out of town in two days. And I've still to follow up on around 20 emails that require some kind of action. That's a typical day.

A non-typical day is one where I don't do my To Do list. I'm rushed and I'm hurried, and I'm unsure of what's happening because I haven't invested the time in the morning to plan it out.

Here's the thing. Does everything on my plan get done? No. But, you can pretty well sure fire guarantee that if I don't plan, it's also not going to get done. I figure if I make a plan I've got a good chance of getting half way through.

So, a typical day for me is doing these things and recording something. I also recorded a video for my YouTube channel today. I'll do that every couple of days, given the opportunity.

But, everyone's day is different, yes? Here's my best suggestion for any day. Go to bed the night before and know what you'll be doing immediately that you wake up. Go to bed the night before and have a plan for the first 90 minutes of the next day. That's a good plan.

 Go to bed the night before and have a plan for the first 90 minutes of the next day. That's a good plan.

What is the most you've ever earned at once? i.e. one transaction, one business sale, speaking engagement?

$40,000 or thereabouts. Hey, it came from one speaking gig. It wasn't just for the engagement of being there. It wasn't for one sale. It was for a number of sales of product that I had on offer, one of those pitch fest deals. I don't like them, but I do do them from time to time to the right audience.

Before preparing my presentation that week I had asked participants what they wanted to hear, what they wanted to see, and what they wanted to perhaps buy and take home with them. I created something custom just for them. I sold $40,000 dollars of it that day, over $100,000 dollars of it that week.

Is that uncommon? Yes. Does it happen often? No, it's never happened since. But I do repeat that formula time and time again just with different amounts. It's a good formula to follow, don't you think? Ask people what they want, and then give it to them. Definitely.

What can people do to stay on track, especially when times get tough?

- Get help

- Ask for favors

- Surround yourself with friends

- Remember the important things in life

- Accept that success in business isn't the be all and end all.

It's just one of many things that we should be doing as we walk this planet.

It's a poor reflection on our current society that we spend eight to ten (some poor people 12) hours a day working that we might have a better life. Pathetic. It's a better that we invest our time wisely, be that six, eight, or ten hours from time to time to earn a good enough income to enjoy our life with family and friends.

That's the key to happiness. Surround yourself with people who make you feel good, who make you feel great. Yes, you can do that in your business. Yes, you can do that speaking.

It's been over 30 years since I first stood on stage. I've walked platforms from the local community hall to the United Nations building in New York. I've presented in front of audiences of ten and 10,000.

No single thing has ever made me happier in my life than being in the arms of a beautiful woman. Feeling loved, feeling wanted, feeling needed, feeling desired. These things overshadow any achievement in my life.

So, in those difficult times these are the things that I like to be reminded of, the things that are truly important. Do you want to know how to stay on track? Remember why you're working in the first place. Set your list of things to do and then just do them. Nike got it right. *Just do it.* Go out and do it now.

 Nike got it right. Just do it. Go out and do it now.

Sonny was born in Berkshire, United Kingdom in 1988 and grew up in Malawi (East Africa) before moving to Sydney, Australia.

Upon completion of a degree in Business and after three years' experience with Ernst & Young, Sonny felt his passion lay elsewhere. He took a few months off to attain clarity and direction… and never returned to the corporate environment.

Trish Springsteen

Trish Springsteen

Don't Try To Be Anyone Else

Trish was born in Rabaul, Papua New Guinea in 1956. She didn't stay there long — her parents moved to Australia when she was six months old. She grew up in Canberra, completed her Associate Diploma in Medical Records Administration and met her husband Peter in Melbourne. They moved to Brisbane where she completed her bachelor degree in Business (Health Administration) while working full-time and looking after two children and a husband.

Like most 18-year-olds, Trish left high school thinking she would have the world at her feet. Reality struck in her first job in a travel agency. No one told her she would have to speak to people, attend network meetings and even present. She used to find the nearest pot plant to hide behind, look frantically for the exit and leave within ten minutes. This did not bode well for her career.

Then Trish found a mentor who grabbed her, shook her and shoved her out onto a speaking stage. It was the best thing that ever happened to her.

Today she is managing director and co-founder of "Trischel" — where she passionately creates confident communicators. As well as being a professional speaker and author of many articles and books on the importance of effective communication for business, she is a recognised expert in the field of communication training.

Having personally experienced the fear of public speaking and being lost for words when facing questions, Trish is passionate about helping others conquer their fear of speaking and communication. Most importantly, she loves what she does and has fun doing it.

Do you suffer from nerves and if so how do you manage them?

I still suffer from nerves — the difference is now I know how to manage them and use that nervous energy to create the WOW factor for my presentations. I turn those nerves into excitement to give me the adrenaline to step up and be my best. I believe that the day I don't have nerves will be the day that my presentations become bland.

One of the key factors in managing those nerves is a matter of having a change of mindset — instead of thinking I'm nervous, I think I'm excited to be here, excited to participate and excited to share with my audience.

The other key factor is the use of visualisation. I prepare my speeches then sit down and in my mind go through every aspect of the presentation — from being introduced, to giving the speech, to hearing the applause and sitting down. I'm programming my mind for success. It works — took me awhile to accept and believe but now it really works.

And then I breathe — deep, deep breaths. Before I start speaking, I'll take three deep breaths — I find this gives me the oxygen I need to start and it gives me a 'centred' feeling. I'm in control.

What do you believe are the top 5 attributes of a successful speaker?

- **Being you** — in my opinion it's essential to be yourself when presenting — don't try to be anyone else. Being you brings validity and trust to the presentation. An audience can easily pick up on anything false. Be natural.

- **Being prepared** — not only knowing your presentation but also having the confidence to overcome any setbacks. Knowing your venue, where you are speaking. Being flexible if your equipment breaks down and having backups and alternatives ready to go. I guess you could say having confidence in you.

- **Knowing your audience** — a successful speaker takes the time to ask questions, to know who the audience are, what they want. They make that connection with the audience. Part of this is knowing what goal you want to achieve as a speaker — what is the message or outcome you want them to take away?

- **Good stage presence** — move competently on the stage or speaking area. Own the area and have a confident, controlled persona.

- **Total Package** — for me this is adding the body language, gestures, eye contact and voice to enhance your verbal message. Great speakers do it so well there's no demarcation line. The audience sees the total package, relates and connects with them on all levels.

What kind of training/development did you undertake to become the speaker you are today?

I was lucky to have a friend who dragged me to a Toastmasters meeting. This is what prodded me to begin my journey. I was fortunate to be part of a club that had good mentors and trainers. I got the basics of speaking, the spark and interest that wanted me to go further.

This would have meant nothing if I hadn't had the courage and friends who pushed me to step up and take opportunities that came my way. I pushed my boundaries, entered competitions, took on leadership roles and presented training. This gave me the confidence to step outside the Toastmasters arena and explore speaking opportunities in the "real" world.

Experience and being prepared to accept failure and learn from the experience and the mistakes has been a vital component. If you want to become a good speaker you need to step up at every opportunity, speak, learn and then repeat.

Mentors who will give you honest feedback, support you, brush you off and then set you back on your journey are invaluable. I had and still have some wonderful supportive mentors.

Be open to seminars and workshops given by other good speakers. I learned a lot from these seminars. One very important thing I learned was don't try to be them — listen to the gold nuggets of information, absorb what works for you and leave the rest.

How did you build you confidence as a speaker?

Experience and take advantage of every opportunity that comes your way. Just getting up and speaking. Whether it was just to say a few words of introduction or to give a speech it helped me to realise that the floor was not going to open up and swallow me. Every speech I gave I learned from and every speech I gave showed me that the audience wanted to hear from me — they weren't going to throw tomatoes!

Accepting that I didn't have to be perfect — I just had to be me and share my message — this was a big breakthrough for me. My confidence grew once I had acknowledged and accepted this.

The positive feedback I received from audiences also helped build my self-confidence. It showed me I was able to speak and they wanted to hear.

Experience and take advantage of every opportunity that comes your way.

How do you customise your presentation to meet the needs of the audience?

Preparation is a vital component for me. I ask a lot of questions beforehand to get a feel for the audience I'll be presenting to.

I like to know how many I'm speaking to — if it's a small group I may be able to have more interaction — if it's a large group I may add a PowerPoint presentation.

The dynamics of the group will assist me in creating my presentation — are they business people, what are they looking to get out of the presentation, are they small business owners, sole traders, working from home versus part of teams in large corporations? The answers to these questions ensure my presentation meets the needs of the audience and connects with them.

Is the audience all male, all female or is there a mix? A very important question to answer — the words, tone and even the way I present may subtly change depending on the mix.

Being flexible is important — I need to be able to connect immediately and read the audience. Even with asking questions beforehand I may find, when giving the presentation, I need to tweak it to meet the audience's needs right there and then. I try, if I'm able, to mingle with the audience before giving my presentation just to check if I'm on the right track with the aims and goals of my presentation. This is a good way to get a feel for the audience.

Do you have a product, program or other offering that you present for sale at speaking events? Do you recommend this for new speakers?

I have a print book co-authored with my business partner. I also offer appropriate programmes depending on the event I'm speaking at.

These are workshops with an online training programme and a video programme.

If you're able to get a book written — it's very valuable towards credibility and can be offered for sale. You probably won't make much from the sales of the book — it's more about advertising and promoting who you are.

For a new speaker — I wouldn't panic too much about having something straight off. Get a few speaking events as practice, develop your skills and get a product developed while you're doing it. Basically, don't hold off speaking just because you have not yet produced a product. Start and then value add as soon as you can.

Don't hold off speaking just because you have not yet produced a product. Start and then value add as soon as you can.

What's your advice for a new and emerging speaker to find 'guest' speaker spots?

Put together a speaker's profile and send it out to your local network organisations. There are many around and most, if not all, are looking for guest speakers. Do not expect to be paid straight off — you need to develop confidence, build relationships and you need to be known.

Contact clubs such as Rotary, Lions and Chambers of Commerce — they're often looking for speakers for their meetings. If you're looking for experience you could also become a volunteer speaker for the Heart Foundation — they have a specific topic you speak on but it can be worthwhile just to get in front of an audience.

Some groups such as Women's Network Australia have a speaker's section where they regularly post groups looking for speakers.

Use social media such as Facebook, LinkedIn and Meetup to source groups and networks that might be looking for speakers — you can build relationships here.

The more speaking experience you get the more refined you can make your presentation. You will be able to gather testimonials and you will become known. At each presentation, remember to always ask if anyone knows other groups who maybe wishing to book a speaker. Always ask for referrals.

As you gain experience, you can then start sending your speaker's kit to event organisers, conference organisers and speakers bureaus.

 The more speaking experience you get the more refined you can make your presentation.

Did you always know the career path you wanted to take? If not, where did you start from and how did you make the change?

Having a speaking and training career never entered my mind when I first left high school. If you had said to any of my friends back then that I would be a professional speaker and trainer they would have laughed. In fact I spent 20 years being afraid to step up and speak. I dodged and missed out on opportunities in my career because I had a fear of speaking.

I started out in the travel industry, progressed through the medical indemnity field, funeral industry and energy industries. Until a mentor grabbed me shook me and convinced me that I could speak. That mentor invited me to join Toastmasters where I took my first steps on the public speaking journey. As I progressed on this journey, an exciting thing happened — I found I loved speaking and training, I discovered I was good at it and, more importantly, my confidence built.

Six years ago I co-founded our training business and I started speaking professionally. I love being able to help people expand and develop.

I especially love sharing my story so others can see that anyone can develop speaking skills and become a public speaker. It took me over 20 years to discover my passion, I hope through my speaking career I can help others so that it doesn't take them that long to have the confidence to step up and share their passion, business idea or message.

What business are you in and what services does it offer?

My business is creating confident communicators. I'm managing director and Co-founder of Trischel — an innovative communication training company specialising in innovative public speaking workshops and corporate communication workshops for both the private and public sector. We provide community workshops and work in corporations delivering training in communication, public speaking, presentation skills, networking, customer service, gender communication, leadership, leadership for women and personal development. Our training for staff, managers and directors empowers companies to increase revenue while building credibility.

I work with individuals, coaching them to improve their communication and presentation skills. My coaching gives clients the confidence and skills to increase their interpersonal skills, handle media interviews, TV interviews and confidently appear on video to effectively communicate and deliver charismatic speeches and presentations.

I'm a professional speaker and trainer for seminars, conferences, keynotes, meetings, MC for events and dinners, facilitator for discussion groups and meeting and can act as an independent Chairman for meetings.

Did you have to change your mindset surrounding public speaking? If so, how did you do it?

Yes, I did have to change my mindset regarding public speaking. I had to realise and accept I was good at speaking and that I actually could get up in front of people. From someone who had a fear of speaking and had let that fear limit his or her opportunities over the years, that was a very big change in my mindset.

When I first started, I really had no self-confidence or self-belief. Why would anyone want to listen to me — what could I say that would be valuable to an audience?

It was hard the first few times getting up and speaking but I found that the more I did the more confident I became. What really helped was the feedback from the audience and from my mentors. The first few positive testimonials that come can really boost your confidence. When you continue to get good testimonials you just have to believe in yourself.

The next step is to accept that belief and take ownership — make it part of who you are. Feedback from mentors who highlight your positives and nudge you to be yourself only more so help to build a solid foundation of self-belief.

Importantly, you must also have a mindset that accepts it's okay to fail, as long as you learn and grow from that failure. Occasionally you will have the not so perfect presentation — train yourself to concentrate on the positives not the 5 or 10 minutes where it may not have quite been to your usual standard. Learn, incorporate, try it out, accept it and take ownership, grow and repeat.

Affirmations work well for me plus positive reinforcement. Today I'm very comfortable with who I am and I know that I'm a good speaker who does have a message and I enjoy and have fun doing what I do. I continually challenge myself to improve, tweak and polish all my presentations.

Have a mindset that accepts it's okay to fail, as long as you learn and grow from that failure.

Do you continue to practice your personal development even now?

I absolutely continue with my own self-development. If you don't, you stagnate. To be a good speaker you need to be always checking and seeing where you can improve, what could you change to do slightly different that may improve what you are doing.

Knowledge is power: self-knowledge and self-development provides you with the power to shine and continually offer the best to your audiences.

> *Knowledge is power and self-knowledge and self-development provides you with the power to shine and continually offer the best to your audiences.*

Is there a significant quote or saying that you live by?

I have a couple of quotes that work for me and resonate with my passion for communication and self-development.

My favourite communication quote is by Sir Richard Branson: "If the best real estate is all about 'location, location, location', then the mantra for running the best business has got to be 'communication, communication, communication'." For me this highlights the importance of communication in business and in personal life — it underpins everything we do but is the one thing least addressed.

My favourite motivation quote is by Marvin Phillips: "The difference between try and triumph is just a little oomph!" I love this because it encourages me to keep trying. This is supported by another quote I love by Harriet Beecher Stowe: "When you get into a tight place never give up for that is just the place and time that the tide will turn."

I have a saying that a mentor of mine passed on. I find this wonderful when preparing for a presentation — it calms me and puts me into a positive frame of mind to shine — "this is simple, this is easy, this is fun." And it really is.

What is the first step that someone could take if they decided to follow in your footsteps today?

Do it now — don't wait. Don't procrastinate because you will always find the time is just not quite right. Take the risk — push yourself outside your comfort zone and get up and speak. Put yourself in the way of opportunity and don't let it go by you — reach out grab on and hold on for the most exciting, challenging but enjoyable journey of your life.

Really know what your message is — be clear about what you are doing and why you are doing. Be comfortable with who you are and be natural.

 Don't be afraid to aim high — hey, if you don't quite get there you still will be great.

What do you think stops people from achieving the level of success they desire?

The biggest thing that stops people achieving is fear — fear of failure, fear of not being good enough, even fear of success. What would happen if I actually succeeded? When faced with setbacks — audiences that may have been difficult, problems finding speaking engagements — a lot of people let their self-doubt grow bigger and bigger and in the end, it is just easier to give up.

Don't be afraid to aim high — hey, if you don't quite get there you still will be great.

Resources

The Ultimate Elevator Pitch

Attending a property auction, I walked through the house one last time before bidding started. I was mentally placing my furniture when another buyer walked in.

A full three seconds later the realisation hit me. Right there in front of me was the Chief Information Officer whose gatekeeper I hadn't been able to bypass. We had been introduced by one of his people but it had gone no further. I impulsively called his name and as he turned, I smiled, stuck out my hand and introduced myself saying our paths had crossed in business.

He smiled politely not remembering me at all: "Oh, yes of course. What is it you do?"

And there was my elevator moment. True story!

Your moment arrives, your chance of a lifetime, face-to-face with your ideal client and you have roughly 30 seconds to make a powerful first impression and say something that communicates exactly what you do interestingly enough so that they want to know more.

It's called the Elevator Pitch, except I wasn't in an elevator, which taught me something else — the elevator pitch can be used anywhere, anytime to garner interest, make connections, start a conversation, kick off the sales process or simply to introduce yourself and your business in a highly professional manner rather than a strangled, "aargh, um I'm uh, you know, like...um," guaranteed to end any encounter before it begins.

There are 7 keys to the ultimate elevator pitch:

1. The elevator pitch is a sound bite only to start a conversation, not your whole business plan. 30 seconds max.

2. It's all about them, not about you. Tell them WHO you help and the ISSUES they are dealing with and WHAT they get from working with you.

3. No waffle. Be short, sharp, pithy. Make every word count.

4. Don't talk about the processes you will follow. That comes much later.

5. Prepare a number of different versions, corner unsuspecting colleagues, friends, family and try them out to get feedback on which one is best.

6. Rehearse it until it rolls off your tongue fluently.

7. Refine as the business, goals or target market changes.

The 5 questions to developing your Elevator Pitch

In writing your initial responses to the questions below, ideally each would be only a few words. However if it is your first time doing this you may draft answers that are half a page long; go back and look for the key words, what is it that really stands out for you that speaks to the heart of what your business is really about.

1. Who do you help through your work?

2. What qualifies them to work with you?

3. What service do you actually perform?

4. **What's the chief result you attain for your client?**

5. **Why is that result important to them?**

Let's look at a couple of examples:**Example 1: Value For Life — Presentation Skills Consultancy www.valueforlife.com.au**

1. **Who do you help through your work?**
   Leaders, executives and their teams

2. **What qualifies them to work with you?**
   Large corporates, blue chip organisations

3. **What service do you actually perform?**
   Simplify their business communications

4. **What's the chief result you attain for your client?**
   Clarity, impact and memorability of key messages

5. **Why is that result important to them?**

   Makes it easy for their stakeholders to make more favourable business decisions.

Now put it all together...

I work with leaders, executives and their teams in blue chip organisations simplifying their business communications. This boosts clarity, impact and memorability of key messages, making it easy for their stakeholders to make more favourable business decisions.

Example 2: IT Success — IT Sourcing and Selection Firm www.itsuccess.com.au

IT Success is a leading edge Australian sourcing and selection firm who have stepped outside what is considered normal recruitment practices. They never use job boards, and never advertise. Instead they source IT talent consistently and build rock solid relationships so that when the right opportunity presents itself, they already know who is at the top of their game and will seamlessly complement an organisation's culture. They can then suggest a perfect fit for their client.

1. **Who do you help through your work?**
   IT professionals at all levels of seniority

2. **What qualifies them to work with you?**
   They must be the best IT industry talent at the top of their game

3. **What service do you actually perform?**
   Search & selection recruitment process for our clients

4. **What's the chief result you attain for your client?**
   Locate the right candidate not the best applicant

5. **Why is that result important to them?**
   Our clients always have the right people in the right roles ensuring the business continues to fulfil the promises it has made to its customers.

And bringing it all together:

> We provide a strategically astute search and selection process for IT Professionals, **regardless** of seniority, so that **our** clients consistently have the right people in place and can continue to fulfil **their** promises

And in case you're wondering what happened after the auction — yes I got the business. Neither of us bought the house.

The Five Minute Phobia Cure

The Five Minute Phobia Cure was developed by Dr. Roger Callahan, a successful psychologist and founder of Thought Field Therapy. Dr. Callahan sadly passed away in November 2013 and his Five Minute Phobia Cure is reprinted here with the generous permission of his wife Joanne M Callahan the current President/CEO of Callahan Techniques, Ltd. To further explore (and benefit from) Dr. Callahan's work, please visit www.rogercallahan.com

Public speaking is one of, if not the, most common phobia experienced. As mentioned earlier in this book I was headed out to speak on the topic of fear and the Five Minute Phobia Cure and considering the considerable discomfort I experienced when in front of any audience larger than a single person, I felt I should at least do the exercise myself so I had a real case study to work with.

Working myself into a lather whilst visualising myself in front of an audience was a surprisingly easy task. No wonder I was unnerved by speaking if just a simple picture in my head could have me at near hysteria.

I worked through the exercise once, checked in and found myself still at a level of 3 out of 10. That is still too high so I did the exercise again. When I checked in again by visualising the picture that had had me in a sweat only a short time earlier, there was nothing except a sense of calm.

The gig itself went unbelievably well. As I stood to speak, I could feel a knot of the old fear in the pit of my stomach. Ordinarily at this point, the point of having been introduced and now all eyes are on me, the knot would explode and become a pulsating sea of terror coursing throughout my body. Not this time. The knot felt as if it were a ball and my body was a pinball machine, it bounced around seeking something to latch onto and there was nothing. I can honestly say, I enjoyed speaking to that group and that enjoyment has stayed with me.

The Five Minute Phobia Cure is used primarily for phobias such as fear of public speaking or flying but I have found it works extremely well on anything that has extreme emotions involved such the fear of rejection or even a fear of success.

The steps for the Five Minute Phobia Cure are outlined below. It is used primarily for phobias but works well on anything that has extreme emotions involved such as fear of speaking in front of groups, fear of success, fear of rejection etc.

How it works exactly is not known but it is believed to change the charge on stored files in your neurology affecting every place you store memory — visual, auditory, feelings, intuition and logic.

First of all, tap the heel of your hand 35 times — refer to Diagram A below*.

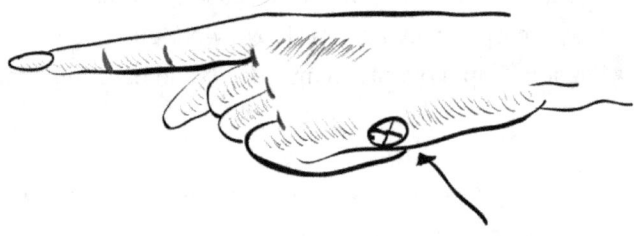

Step 1

Close your eyes and place your hands in your lap. Put yourself into the fear by imagining or remembering yourself in a situation with whatever

---

* images provided drawn by Alma of Peacefulart.

it is that you fear. Feel the emotions associated with it, hear what you'd be hearing, see what you'd be seeing. Make the picture as bright and clear as you can.

On a scale of 1-10 with 10 being the fear at its worst, rate your level of fear. Whilst 10 is ideal, get as close as you can. There is no need to hurry through this step. The clearer the picture, the better the result.

Step 2

Tap yourself under the eyes 35 times with 2 fingers of each hand — refer to Diagram B below.

Step 3

Next, begin tapping the **left** hand as shown in Diagram C below.

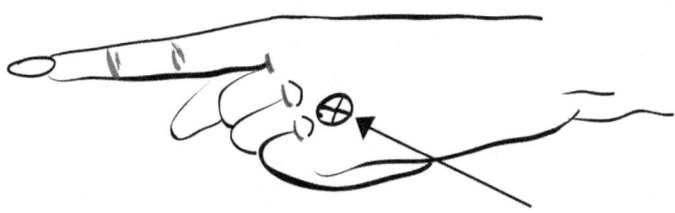

Continue to tap the point on your left hand through this step.

Open your eyes and while keeping your head straight, look to the lower left then to the lower right.

Move eyes around in a circle one way, return to centre. Move eyes around the other way and return to centre.

Close your eyes, open your eyes, hum a song of your choice (*Happy Birthday* is a great choice as it's simple and familiar), then count out loud slowly to 10.

Cease tapping and return your hands to your lap.

Step 4

Close your eyes and again visualise the fear inducing experience

Rate the fear on a scale of 1-10. If the number is 3 or above, repeat steps 1-4.

Step 5

Sometimes although the fear is gone, it can be challenging to believe that something that once had such a powerful hold over you has dissipated so quickly and for that reason if you are in any doubt whatsoever repeat the entire process again…just to be sure.

It is highly unlikely the fear will ever return but if you feel that it has then simply repeat the process.

Preparing Your Speakers Kit

Once you begin marketing yourself as a speaker, sooner or later you will be faced with someone asking you to send them your information. By information they mean your speakers kit. This should be a polished document that showcases your knowledge and capabilities and makes it clear to the person considering engaging you that you will be a worthy contributor to their event.

Although you will write the first draft, it is well worth the investment to hire a copywriter to add that extra polish.

While this is the format I use, it is not by any means the only option available to you. A little research will no doubt uncover others that you can adapt to suit.

What to include in your speakers kit:

1. **Photograph:** a professional headshot is appropriate; a family snapshot of you in a bikini is not. Your headshot should show you smiling, facing front on with a neutral background. To have professional photographs taken look for a photographer who specialises in branding headshots. For Melbourne based readers check out the incredible talent of Ramona Lever at www.brandingheadshots.com.au

2. **Professional Biography:** this is an introduction to you so make it count. Share some background information, professional experience as well as a little bit of personal to show your human side — your family, hobbies, passions, goals. Whatever you choose to share should make a prospective audience connect with you.

There are 20 professionally edited examples in this book for you to use as a guide.

3. **What types of presentations do you give?**

    1. Keynote speeches

    2. Conferences

    3. Seminars.

How long do you speak for?

Are your speeches adaptable?

Pulling this all together, you might draft the information into your actual speakers kit as follows:

Types of presentations:

- Keynote and conferences

- Breakfast, lunch and evening seminars

- 30-90 minutes

- All topics can be adapted to workshop format.

4. **Speaking subject and blurb:** prepare 4 — 6 topics with a headline (what your presentation is called) and up to eight lines of text that sells the content of your presentation. Following are two real life examples to give you some ideas around formatting:

Change the Conversation: Change Your Life

So often we negatively limit our progress by putting the brakes on ourselves, our dreams, goals, ambitions, relationships, careers, finances and our personal growth.

Yet we have within our grasp the power to release those brakes and positively accelerate our way to a compelling future.

Explore the simple strategies that will release the brakes so you can change your life and learn how to apply these strategies straight away for maximum effect.

An engaging and motivating topic that will inspire you to start living the life of your dreams.

Life On Purpose

People in business have key performance indicators to track their business performance and most can tell you straight away exactly what those are.

Yet what key performance indicators have you put in place for the other 87.5% of your life?

People spend more time planning a holiday than they do planning the rest of their lives! If you don't know where you're going then you'll end up someplace else.

Setting goals immediately elevates you from going through the motions to pursuing a journey of fulfillment. Decide what you want, focus upon it and start living life on purpose now.

5. **What can the organisers expect from you?** This is another bit of salesmanship, a few key points that highlight what you will deliver.

For example:

- Entertaining, engaging and relevant content

- Well researched and prepared content specific to your needs

- No death by PowerPoint!

- Challenging, thought-provoking experiences

- Professional, original and individually tailored presentations.

6. **How can you be contacted?** Include your phone number, email address and other forms of connection such as your Facebook page, LinkedIn profile address, twitter account and website address.

Again, it's well worth engaging a copywriter or editor to cast a professional eye over your speakers kit, if only to ensure spelling and grammar are accurate. Consider for a moment your absolute mortification upon discovering you have inadvertently advertised yourself as a *pubic* speaker. It's too late once you have pressed the send button.

Claiming Your Free Bonus Gifts

Many contributors have generously offered not only their wisdom and insights but also free bonus gifts to you, the reader. Here's what you'll receive when you visit our website at www.presenttthisbook.com:

Free gift 1: ($97 value) Mindfield: The Success Principles of Insanely Great Presenters. If you're serious about becoming the best presenter, the best speaker you can be then you need to start here with the basics. This e-book will unlock the secret strategies of the great allowing you to close the gap between you and the person on stage that you want to be.

Free gift 2: ($50 value) The Doctor Is In. From time to time we all need someone to lean on, to listen to us and help ease the burden, whatever that is. Dr Alegado is offering all readers a 50% discount on a 30-minute initial consultation.

Free Gift 3: ($350 value) WOW! Bonus access to the coaching used by leading internet entrepreneurs, family business leaders, corporate executive leaders and company directors. Contact Danny via his website www.theinnovationcoach.com.au and mention this book to receive a free bonus 20-minute Skype based Business Innovation mentoring session.

Free Gift 4: ($495 value) Build, Elevate and Accelerate — Video Training Series. Fiona is an expert in helping women leverage their natural strengths and skills to create powerful career positioning now and in the future. Now you can access one of Fiona's key trainings in which she teaches the tools you need to build and maintain a successful, fulfilling and rewarding career. "Build Your Influence, Elevate Your Personal Brand and Accelerate Your Leadership Skills" is a video training series Fiona has designed for her clients and you can access it for free.

Free Gift 5: ($97 value) MP3 Red Carpet Secrets. Julie-Anne has travelled the world leading fresh and entertaining training programs that inspire thousands of emerging leaders to be bold, sassy and dynamic in life and business. Listening to this valuable audio will give you the Five Red Carpet Secrets To Communicate Like a Superstar. You'll also discover why Brad Pitt plays outgoing characters to break away from his shyness. Come behind the scenes with Julie-Anne as she combines her expertise as mindset, body language and NLP trainer with the secrets she learned as a top television producer. There's never been a better time to be brilliant now.

Free Gift 6: ($499 value) Don't Get Hacked. Have your internet presence checked today for security holes with this free vulnerability assessment service. With more than 60,000 different security vulnerabilities identified and logged in our database, we will check your web-server, mail-server and firewall. And if your business accepts credit cards, we are authorised by VISA and Mastercard to check for security problems related to credit card handling. Keep your business safe.

Free gift 7: ($27 value) Overcoming Common Mistakes. Do you worry about making mistakes on stage? Karen has prepared a report for you on the seven most common mistakes made so you can more easily avoid them and enjoy your time in the spotlight.

Free Gift 8: ($97 value) Comedy Gold. Make your presentation funnier by listening to this audio recording that explores Kate's top tips for comedy gold. This recording provides a better understanding of what makes something funny so you can add original humour to your presentation. Adding humor to your presentation can help build rapport faster, stop the audience staring at you like you are on TV and assist you to communicate your message more effectively.

Free gift 9: ($39 value) Storytelling Lessons from Rural Kenya. From the heart of rural Kenya comes a real life story that will open your eyes to what's really possible. Packed full of valuable lessons this powerful tale will boost your public speaking confidence, skyrocket your happiness at work, engage and inspire your team (and family) into action and importantly inspire you to join the important global movement of 'being the change.'

Free gift 10: ($14.97 value) What do Vegans Eat? Dispelling the myth that vegans aren't healthy and eat boring and bland food, Leigh-Chantelle is focussed on putting the fun into vegan health education. This visually appealing look at the many delicious food options available to vegans today is delivered in Leigh-Chantelle's own unique, charming, no-fuss style.

Free Gift 11: ($47 value) Relaxation Guided Meditation. As a presenter, you inspire, empower and move your audience into meaningful action, helping them get the results they want. To support you in that, Lisa has created a short, guided meditation to enable you to instantly relax your body, clear your mind, open your heart and step into your most authentic self and powerful presence before you go on stage. Enjoy!

Free gift 12: ($39 value) Six Secrets to Build a Business You Love. Critical to the success of a business is attracting clients. This audio download talks you through the low cost strategies to bring in business that will increase your income so you can build the business you love.

Free gift 13: ($279 value) Beyond Your Fears. In addition to being passionate about speaking to audiences of all sizes, Narelle is a master hypnotherapist who has helped hundreds of clients through her powerful visualisation sessions and recordings. She is a master of the mind, and now you too can experience powerful mindset techniques with Narelle guiding you through a 45-minute live process that will leave you feeling relaxed and confident.

Free gift 14: ($19.97 value) Fabulous at 50. Pat knows what it takes to turn bad health into good health and maintain it long term. Fit, Fun and Fabulous at Fifty is a simple, easy to follow guide to achieving the ideal 'middle' during middle age. Pat's Top 50 Tips to Fat Loss e-book provides simple and easy strategies to help you shed those excess kilos without breaking the bank.

Free gift 15: ($57 value) Ten Tips For Improving Your Presentation. Resources at your fingertips when preparing your presentation are invaluable. This useful e-book assists in defining the purpose of your presentation and provides some pointers to knowing your audience and venue in addition to adding value by using props, body language and voice. And to help you prepare for your next presentation, download the template and checklist.

To download your free gifts simply visit the dedicated webpage below:

www.picturethemnakedbook.com.au

The intellectual property rights associated with each of the bonus gifts belong to the respective creators and as such unauthorised distribution, modification or copying is prohibited without the express written permission of the creator.

All free bonus gifts offered are current at the time of printing.

About the Contributors

The most enormous thank you goes to all the contributors without whom this book would not have been possible. Many of them have their own books and products. For more information, they would be pleased to hear from you directly.

Mindset Consulting

Name: Dr Aileen Alegado
Phone: +61 405 159 755
Email: aileen@mindsetconsulting.org.au
Website: www.mindsetconsulting.org.au

The Innovation Coach

Name: Danny Davis
Email: info@dannydavis.com.au
Website: www.dannydavis.com.au

Fiona Craig Consulting — Love your Work

Name: Fiona Craig
Phone: +61 1300 051 113
Email: Fiona@fionacraig.com.au
Website: www.fionacraig.com.au

Be Brilliant Now

Name: Julie-Anne Black
Phone: +61 403 577 553
Email: hello@bebrilliantnow.com
Website: www.bebrilliantnow.com
Books: *Who Do You Want to Become, Be Brilliant Now*

Name: Jesper Jurcenoks **Critical Watch**
Phone: +1 866 525 8680
Email: jesper.jurcenoks@criticalwatch.com
Website: www.criticalwatch.com

Name: Karen Ostenried **Get On Stage**
Phone: +61 3 57861053
Email: info@getonstage.com.au
Website: www.getonstage.com.au
Books: *10 Secrets For Stage Success*

Name: Kate Burr **Sore Cheeks Comedy Pty Ltd**
Email: Kate@kateburr.com
Website: www.kateburr.com
Books: *Ickety Uckety Umm — Nursery Rhymes for New Mums*

Name: Kristy Moore **Hand Up Australia**
Phone: +61 414 424 304
Email: kristy.moore@handupaustralia.com
Website: www.handupaustralia.com

Name: Lara Shannon **Eco TV, Ecochick**
Phone: +61 415 076 015
Email: lara@larashannon.com
Website: www.larashannon.com and www.ecochick.com

Name: Leigh-Chantelle **Epicentre Equilibrium**
Email: contact@epicentreequilibrium.com
Website: www.epicentreequilibrium.com, www.leigh-chantelle.com, www.vivalavegan.net
Books: *There's a Vegan in the Kitchen: Viva La Vegan's Easy & tasty Plant Based Recipes, What do Vegans Eat?*

Name:	Lisa Page	**Soul Satisfaction For Women**
Email:	lisa@soulsatisfactionforwomen.com	
Website:	www.soulsatisfactionforwomen.com	

Name:	Maureen Bell	**Speak With Presence**
Phone:	+61 421 070 987	
Email:	Maureen@speakwithpresence.com.au	
Website:	www.speakwithpresence.com.au	

Name:	Mireille Ryan	**Health Guru Industries**
Phone:	+61 7 5593 8823	
Email:	mireille@healthyguruindustries.com.au	
Website:	www.mireilleryan.com	

Name:	Narelle Lee	**The Performance Masters**
Phone:	+61 401 141 600	
Email:	narelle@theperformancemasters.com.au	
Website:	www.theperformancemasters.com.au	
Books:	Now We're Talking…Health for Mature Women; Financial Freedom Explained — your guide to managing your finances and your life.	

Name:	Pat Rae	**Pat Rae Personal Training**
Phone:	+61 414 654 372	
Email:	pat@patrae.com	
Website:	www.patrae.com	
Books:	Ten Step Plan to Healthy Living, My Fifty Top Tips to Fat Loss, PRPT Training Diary	

Name:	Paul Barrs	**Paul Barrs Publishing**
Email:	paul@paulbarrs.com	
Website:	www.paulbarrs.com	

Name:	Trish Springsteen	**Trischel**
Phone:	+61 7 5433 1105	
Email:	trish@trischel.com.au	
Website:	www.trischel.com.au and www.coachingpublicspeaking.com	
Books:	*Learning Can Be fun* — *Trischel's Book of Blogs, Creating Confident Communicators* (e-book)	

www.ingramcontent.com/pod-product-compliance
Lightning Source LLC
Chambersburg PA
CBHW071902290426

44110CB00013B/1248